INTERNATIONAL
FINANCE
CORPORATION

DISCUSSION PAPER NUMBER 21

Radical Reform
in the Automotive Industry

Policies in Emerging Markets

Peter O'Brien
Yannis Karmokolias

The World Bank
Washington, D.C.

The International Finance Corporation (IFC), an affiliate of the World Bank, promotes the economic development of its member countries through investment in the private sector. It is the world's largest multilateral organization providing financial assistance directly in the form of loan and equity to private enterprises in developing countries.

To present the results of research with the least possible delay, the typescript of this paper has not been prepared in accordance with the procedures appropriate to formal printed texts, and the IFC and the World Bank accept no responsibility for errors. Some sources cited in this paper may be informal documents that are not readily available. The findings, interpretations, and conclusions expressed in this paper are entirely those of the author(s) and should not be attributed in any manner to the IFC or the World Bank or to members of their Board of Executive Directors or the countries they represent. The World Bank does not guarantee the accuracy of the data included in this publication and accepts no responsibility whatsoever for any consequence of their use.

The material in this publication is copyrighted. Requests for permission to reproduce portions of it should be sent to Director, Economics Department, IFC, at the address shown in the copyright notice above. The IFC encourages dissemination of its work and will normally give permission promptly and, when the reproduction is for noncommercial purposes, without asking a fee. Permission to copy portions for classroom use is granted through the Copyright Clearance Center, Inc., Suite 910, 222 Rosewood Drive, Danvers, Massachusetts 01923, U.S.A.

The complete backlist of publications from the World Bank, including those of the IFC, is shown in the annual *Index of Publications,* which contains an alphabetical title list (with full ordering information) and indexes of subjects, authors, and countries and regions. The latest edition is available free of charge from the Distribution Unit, Office of the Publisher, Department F, The World Bank, 1818 H Street, N.W., Washington, D.C. 20433, U.S.A., or from Publications, The World Bank, 66, avenue d'Iéna, 75116 Paris, France.

ISSN: 1012-8069

Library of Congress Cataloging-in-Publication Data

O'Brien, Peter, 1947–
        Radical reform in the automotive industry : policies in emerging
    markets / Peter O'Brien, Yannis Karmokolias.
            p.   cm. — (Discussion paper / International Finance
    Corporation, ISSN 1012-8069 ; no. 21)
        Includes bibliographical references.
        ISBN 0-8213-2806-9
        1. Automobile industry and trade—Developing countries.
    2. Automobile industry and trade—Government policy—Developing
    countries.   I. Karmokolias, Yannis, 1946–   .   II. Title.
    III. Series: Discussion paper (International Finance Corporation) ;
    no. 21.
    HD9710.D452O28   1994
    338.4'76292'091724—dc20   94-8112
                                                                  CIP

Contents

List of Charts

Foreword

This study was inspired by IFC-sponsored round-tables which brought together industry executives and policymakers in South America, South and East Asia, and Central Europe. It offers insights as well as speculation about the future of the fastest-growing automotive markets, those of the developing countries. The industry is important; in several developing countries it has come to play a major role in output, employment and exports. The *leitmotiv* is globalization and what this means for the industry. The study offers far-reaching suggestions. For example, component industries, a much-neglected segment, can thrive and help to generate foreign exchange where car assembly may not succeed. The development of future automotive industries does not need to start with assembly, as has been the case in many countries, but could be based on component manufacturing that might lead later to assembly.

After sketching out major trends, the study outlines the industry's structure and then assesses policies. The concluding chapter speculates about strategic policy perspectives for major developing country markets.

Peter O'Brien is an international industry consultant and Yannis Karmokolias a staff member of IFC's Economics Department who has done extensive work on the automotive industry of developing countries.

Guy Pfeffermann
Director, Economics Department
and Economic Advisor of the Corporation

v

Abstract

The automotive industry has been the subject of considerable research over the years. Practically all such research has dealt with the automotive industry in developed countries that formerly accounted for nearly all production and the bulk of sales. Little attention has been given to the industry in developing countries. Yet, in 1993 the Emerging Markets of Central/Eastern Europe, Asia/Pacific, and Latin America accounted for approximately 19 percent of global vehicle output, twice greater than the share had been in 1985, despite major disruptions in the former USSR and Yugoslavia. Vehicle sales in these countries have recently been growing at least 30 percent annually, much faster than in OECD countries, while exports of both vehicles and components have been substantial.

This paper focusses on the automotive industry in developing countries. It builds on the round-table discussions organized by the International Finance Corporation (IFC) in Brazil, India, Indonesia, and Hungary involving automotive industry executives from the respective regions and from multinational companies, Government policymakers, industry experts and IFC staff. The discussions covered business aspects of the industry, such as technological changes, characteristics of the market place, the changing relationship between suppliers and assemblers, and between multinational and developing country companies; and policy aspects such as macroeconomics, competition, trade regime, local content regulations, and the environment. This paper reviews the main points of the round-table discussions, the major changes that have taken place since then and the implications for developing countries. The core part of the paper reviews the impact of macroeconomic changes on business decisions; regulations governing market structure and production conditions; policy constraints on the growth of domestic demand; trade policy and measures to enhance investment.

I. *Content and Purpose of the IFC-Sponsored Workshops*

The automotive industry can play a dominant role in a country's economic development. In the United States the automotive industry accounts for 5 percent of GNP and 17 percent of industrial employment. In the European Community, 10 percent of industrial employment is tied to vehicle output - in Germany, one job in every six depends on the industry. Mexico now has 9 percent of manufacturing output and 10 percent of manufacturing employment related to vehicle manufacture. In Brazil, where the automotive industry participates only modestly in manufacturing output, 6 percent of the total, and industrial employment, 3 percent of the total, it has a vital role in the country's development because of the substantial linkages to other economic activities. For example, it absorbs 76 percent of aluminum alloys produced in the country, 43 percent of zinc alloys, 36 percent of cast iron, and 18 percent of uncoated flat-rolled iron and steel products. Forward linkages to marketing, repair and maintenance, fuel and lubricants, insurance, shipping, and accessories, are equally extensive.

Because of the industry's potentially major contributions to development, directly and through linkages, many countries that aim to grow through industrialization have regarded the automotive sector as a suitable way to achieve this objective. Since 1956 when IFC was established to promote economic development through support to the private sector, it has financed a variety of investments for both vehicle and component production in many developing countries around the world. The frequency of applications for funding of automotive investment projects accelerated during the eighties as more and more developing country governments supported the development of their automotive industries and private firms, local and multinational, decided to invest in developing countries. Given the very fast pace of change occurring in the industry, its complexity, and the knowledge that protection in many forms often masked the economic realities faced by a project, IFC carried out a study of the industry focussing on developing countries.[1] The study generated requests from the Brazilian automotive industry for IFC to organize a discussion forum in South America so that those directly concerned, that is, vehicle producers and raw materials and component suppliers in that region, would have the opportunity to discuss the study and its findings. At that time the Government of Brazil was contemplating changes in the country's policies dealing with this industry and an event such as the one suggested could be considered appropriate for an exchange of views on the issues facing the industry and how they might be effectively addressed. IFC responded positively to this request.

In May 1990, a two-day round-table discussion was organized in Sao Paulo by IFC and ANFAVEA (Brazil's Automotive Manufacturers Association) attended by most auto assemblers and large component manufacturers in Brazil, some assemblers and suppliers from Argentina and Venezuela, several U.S. and European multinationals, representatives of the Brazilian government, IFC staff and automotive industry experts. The discussions were far reaching, frank and lively. It was an opportunity for many points of view to be expressed and to be understood, if not shared, by those with a different perspective. And there were many perspectives: assemblers/suppliers; South American companies/ multinationals; private sector/Government; investment officers/economists/engineers. The practical aim was for participants to meet outside the more usual, and often adversarial, setting of specific business negotiations. Subsequent to the Sao Paulo event, a number of countries requested IFC to organize similar events. It was decided to cover those regions where the automotive industry was strongest and growing

---

[1] Karmokolias, Yannis *Automotive Industry Trends and Prospects for Investment in Developing Countries*, IFC Discussion Paper No. 7, 1990.

among developing countries. Accordingly, regional round-table-discussions[2] took place in December 1990 in New Delhi (covering South Asia), May 1991 in Jakarta (covering Southeast Asia), and November 1991 in Budapest (covering Central and Eastern Europe).[3]

In each workshop attendance included representatives from:

- Assembly and component producers in the region.

- Government officials directly concerned with the sector.

- International automotive companies, normally those with interests in the countries under review.

- International automotive consultants closely involved with developments in the area.

- IFC staff, primarily those in the engineering and economics departments who have for some time worked on projects and programs in the automotive industry, but also drawing on others engaged in relevant activities for example, privatization programs in Central/Eastern Europe.

The initiative to hold the workshops and the objectives set responded to the concerns both of IFC and of the countries. For IFC the aims were:

- Policy Oriented Dialogue. The automotive industry is an industry where strong conflicts, usually over the degree and type of protection but also stemming from the divergent interests of different entities within the industry, have marked much of the evolution in developing countries.

- Policy Assessment. The automotive industry has for several years been in a state of turmoil, and there is no sign that the near future will differ from the recent past. On the production side the trends to regionalization/globalization have swept the concept of Global Best Practice to center stage. But does the notion of global best practice also apply to policy, in the sense that attainment of specified goals for the automotive industry necessarily requires design and implementation of a particular set of policies? If so, where do the selected countries stand on the policy spectrum? What are the directions of change which should be followed? What obstacles are likely to complicate matters?

- Automotive Industry Trend Assessment and its Policy Applications. The speed of change in the automotive industry compels those who would be successful to analyze continuously the shifts in economic conditions, business strategies and policies elsewhere which condition the likelihood of achieving the policy objectives. The wide range of automotive industry actors present at the workshops offered a splendid opportunity to examine the forces at work and gauge their likely impacts in the countries selected.

- Project Opportunities and Risks. IFC has as its raison d'etre the support of commercially profitable and economically beneficial private sector projects in developing countries. The information

---

[2]   Part of the expenses for the round table discussions were covered by the IFC-Swedish Government (BITS) trust fund.

[3]   Representatives of China's automotive industry attended both the New Delhi and Jakarta events.

generated during and after the workshops provides a frame of reference for project work, some mechanics for monitoring change, and channels of communication which can assist both IFC and potential partners to keep each other informed regarding opportunities and risks.

- **Promotion in Major Countries/Regions.** The two workshops in Asia and that in Latin America were in countries which together account for 60 percent of world population, while the Budapest encounter was in the emerging East European market. From the automotive industry angle there is no doubt that the coverage so obtained permitted focus on all the areas of significant production potential for the 1990s. The breadth of the policy and project challenges in the countries considered, can safely be taken as representative of anything likely to come up in the automotive industry for the foreseeable future.

The developing countries shared these objectives since they recognized that their automotive industry sectors are in delicate periods of transition. They also had the following aims:

- **Industry as the Development Motor.** In all Emerging Markets covered by the workshops, the development effort has been predicated on industrial expansion playing a lead role. Within the industrial sector the automotive industry, because of its potential for forward and backward linkages, occupies a central place. Although other industries might also merit detailed examination, few of them attain the strategic importance of the automotive industry. Hence the success of industrial strategy hinges importantly on its development. In the past some countries tried either a "go-it-alone-path" or one confined to limited regional markets. Political and economic conditions of the 1990s do not allow a continuation of this direction given that development now depends on adequate integration with the international automotive industry economy. In this regard, the workshops facilitated exploration of alternative routes while at the same time, through the diverse composition of the participants, gave a clear signal of a change in attitudes (often at least as important as the policy alterations).

- **Encouragement of New Patterns of Trade.** The integration with external markets, for technologies and equipment as well as for completely built up (CBU) or completely knocked down (CKD) units and components, puts a fresh tint on the automotive balance of payments. Given that all countries recognize the need to set up new ways of handling the foreign exchange impact of automotive trade, detailed discussions with those influential in the markets represent a logical step in the process.

- **The Impetus to Domestic Sales.** The automotive industry, while an important supplier to the middle classes of Emerging Markets, has not been able to expand in any sustained way through reliance on home market sales. But, for socio-political as well as economic reasons, future policy must seek to promote both exports and domestic consumption. To encourage domestic sales yet avoid being swamped by imports requires a careful mix of policies related not only to domestic production but also to trade, pricing, and credit. The workshops gave a chance for these matters to be examined in a comparative setting.

- **Competition Among Locations.** Governments as well as producers are now aware that investors scan a wide spectrum of projects before reaching decisions. So it matters for a country to be visible as a place where economic opportunities are considerable and the commercial/political risks manageable. The structure of deals that can be concluded in any location must be seen to be flexible and open to innovation in their trade, financial and production aspects. International workshops afford a good means to promote this image ("policy trade fairs").

This paper is based on the experience gained and information obtained in the workshops, and on material developed since. Its purposes are:

- To assess the automotive industry situation of the emerging markets in the 1990s.

- To assess the changes made in automotive industry policies in the selected countries and set out possible next steps in the process of transformation.

The structure of the report is as follows: Section II summarizes dominant trends in the world automotive industry economy as of the early/mid 1990s, and situates the selected countries within that context. Section III looks in more detail at what is happening to assembly, component manufacture and demand in the emerging markets. The quantitative and qualitative material used in these two sections give the setting for analysis of policy behavior in Section IV. That material, which is a core part of the study, highlights five dimensions of policy, viz. the impact of macroeconomic changes on business decisions; regulations governing market structure and production conditions; policy constraints on the growth of domestic demand; trade policy; and measures to enhance investment. Section V concludes with a comparative assessment of policy perspectives in the various emerging markets.

II. *Dominant Trends in the World Automotive Industry*

The Vehicle Picture in the 1990s

Table 1 underlines the continued dominance of OECD as the world sales hub - in 1993 it constituted 77 percent of the world car market (reckoned by volume) and even with current slow growth the share by mid decade will still be close to three-quarters. On a value basis the predominance would appear greater. The geographical areas at the core of this study (viz. South America, ASEAN, India, China and Central Europe) absorbed about 8.5 percent of global sales in the early part of the decade and are expected to account for one-tenth by 1995. The critical shift occurring in the early 1990s and likely to become more and more noticeable in the rest of the decade concerns the geographical distribution of the increment to global sales. Even in the late 1980s, the regions classified here as Emerging Markets did not account for as much as one fifth of the increment in any pair of consecutive years. Recent forecasts, however, suggest that these countries now absorb at least 30 percent of year-on-year increases and that this share could approach 35 percent or more by the year 2000.

TABLE 1
WORLD VEHICLE SALES AND DISTRIBUTION BY REGION, 1991 AND 1995

	1991	1995
Sales Volume (mn. units)	47.2	54.0
Shares by Region (percent)		
U.S.A. and Canada	29.3	32.0
Western Europe	32.7	30.3
Japan	15.9	15.2
Mexico	1.4	1.6
South America	2.9	3.3
Republic of Korea	2.3	2.5
Taiwan, China	1.0	1.1
ASEAN	1.8	2.0
India	0.7	1.0
China	1.4	2.0
Eastern Europe (excluding Russia)	1.7	1.6
Other	8.9	7.4

Source: "World Automotive Suppliers", *Financial Times*. June 28, 1993.

The emerging pattern is in sharp contrast to the second half of the 1980s, as Table 2 emphasizes. The sales half of the table highlights:

- The huge surge in leading Asian countries, where registrations more than tripled.

- Sales rises of close to 50 percent or more in the other Asian countries and Hungary (the latter is mostly due to imports in 1990 and 1991).

- The clear difference between Mexico, where registrations doubled, and the stagnation or even major collapse (Venezuela) in the main South American countries.

- The strong performance in Spain and Turkey, also often cited as "yardstick" locations.

Production trends were a fairly good image of changes in sales, though South America did not lag so far behind Asia, while Poland's position slipped back by 50 percent (chiefly due to poor manufacturing performance in 1990/91). Juxtaposition of information given in Tables 1 and 2 points to the following key features of the countries under scrutiny in this report:

- Ranked by current and forecast market size, the order of importance of the selected countries and regions is South America, India and China, ASEAN and Eastern Europe. The trends highlight rapid growth of the world's two mega-countries along with significant expansion in South America. ASEAN and Eastern Europe both appear much less promising in the medium term.

- None of the regions quite matches up to Republic of Korea and Taiwan, China (taken together) as a market, South America is about double Mexico reckoned by sales volume, and Brazil alone somewhat larger.

- Current rank order is virtually the same as regards production. ASEAN manufacturing is currently about double that of India, and 30 percent greater than China.

- If India/China are to sustain the expected rise in domestic sales, both the utilization and scope of production capacity will have to expand fast (unless China decides to permit a sudden import boom, as it did in the late 1980s). A similar conclusion, albeit somewhat scaled-down, holds for the South American leaders (crucially, Brazil).

- While the medium-term outlook set against the world automotive industry map may not suggest dramatic changes are under way, the fact is that the large countries targeted in this study must make very sizeable alterations to their manufacturing bases within a few years. The oft-repeated story of the automotive industry as a world where all the dynamism is concentrated in a handful of OECD locations plus Republic of Korea and Mexico will certainly not be an accurate description of events in the middle and late 1990s.

Vehicle trade, excluding intra EC movements, approximates 11 million units or close to one-third of global sales - of this, the Emerging Markets as a whole export roughly one-tenth. The predominant sources are Republic of Korea, Mexico, Brazil, Czech Republic and Poland. Table 3 summarizes the trade orientation for the selected countries; the figures shown there, in conjunction with other available information, suggest the subsequent observations.

TABLE 2

VEHICLE PRODUCTION AND NEW REGISTRATIONS IN SELECTED COUNTRIES 1991, AND COMPARISONS WITH 1985

REGION/COUNTRY	PRODUCTION (mn. units)		NEW REGISTRATIONS (mn. units)	
	1991	1991/1985 ratio	1991	1991/1985 ratio
I. AMERICAS				
Mexico	0.99	2.5	0.64	2.00
Brazil	0.96	1.0	0.77	1.02
Argentina	0.14	1.0	0.14	0.98
Colombia	0.05	1.2	0.05	1.10
Venezuela	0.04	0.3	0.04	0.30
II. PACIFIC RIM				
Republic of Korea	1.50	3.9	1.05	4.3
Taiwan, China	0.21	1.5	0.55	3.2
Indonesia	0.25	1.8	0.24	1.7
Malaysia	0.17	1.5	0.17	1.5
Thailand	0.21	2.6	0.30	3.5
III. CENTRAL EUROPE AND MEDITERRANEAN				
Spain	2.08	1.3	1.13	1.6
Turkey	0.17	2.8	0.23	3.8
Czech Republic	0.25	1.1	0.24	1.2
Hungary	0.02	1.0	0.16	1.6
Poland	0.18	0.5	0.21	1.1
IV. INDIVIDUAL COUNTRIES				
India	0.34	1.5	.34	1.5
China	0.51	1.2	0.62	1.4

Automotive News, *1992 Market Data Book*. New York.

TABLE 3

FOREIGN TRADE ORIENTATION IN VEHICLE SECTOR, SELECTED COUNTRIES, EARLY 1990s

REGION/COUNTRY	SHARE OF OUTPUT GOING TO EXPORTS (percent)	SHARE OF SUPPLY COMING FROM IMPORTS (percent)
I. AMERICAS		
Mexico	35	5 (20 percent ceiling fixed for 1993 by law)
Brazil	20	negligible
Argentina	< 1	20
Colombia	< 1	4
Venezuela	< 1	4
II. PACIFIC RIM		
Republic of Korea	25	< 1
Taiwan, China	< 1	30
Indonesia	negligible	negligible
Malaysia	10	13
Thailand	7	3
III. CENTRAL EUROPE		
Czech Republic	30	20
Hungary	70 (cv only)	90
Poland	22	12
IV. INDIVIDUAL COUNTRIES		
India	5	< 1
China	negligible	6

Note: Figures are averages of the respective shares in the years 1990-93.
Source: United Nations, International Commodity Trade Data Base; and Automotive Manufacturers' Associations of Argentina, Brazil, Indonesia, India, Malaysia, Thailand.

- Given both the shifts in production location of the late 1980s and the prevailing determination in Europe and Japan to continue management of trade in vehicles, the ratio of global trade to sales is likely to decline.

- The United States remains the major market for emerging country exports but access to it will continue to alter markedly over the next few years, due to fierce competition from the Japanese-owned plants in the United States, the progressive introduction of NAFTA rules and possibly an eventual free trade regime embracing all the Americas. The United States "Big 3" have also started to regain market share: in 1993 GM, Ford and Chrysler together sold three-quarters of cars and light trucks as against two-thirds at the beginning of the decade.

- Latin American countries which adopt aggressive, market oriented policies will be relatively favored by these trends. In the short run, the opportunities will fall to Brazil and Argentina.

- Markets in developing countries remain relatively closed to imports, though they are less hermetic than is often suggested (see Table 3). Gradual opening is occurring in South America, under the impetus of wider-ranging policies of trade compensation and recent drives to promote sub-regional trade. Eastern European import behavior will probably alter substantially in the medium-run, as market liberalization increases in Hungary and Czech Republic. India and China hover around a self-sufficiency level, but the standards of manufacture remain low while dependence on imported components persists.

Automotive Components

In contrast to the ample data on vehicles (especially passenger cars), the component business singularly lacks adequate statistical and qualitative information. The problem is particularly severe for production and for smaller components, whereas trade in larger items is fairly well recorded. Yet the figures and findings which are available point to a number of important policy possibilities in the selected countries.

- Global sales of original equipment manufacture components were estimated at around $500 billion in the early 1990s. Trends towards greater sophistication of parts, and greater outsourcing by assemblers, indicate a growth rate in the middle and late 1990s substantially in excess of that for any other part of the automotive business.

- Replacement market sales are also likely to grow significantly, particularly in a period where new vehicle sales expand at only a moderate rate (see Table 1).

- Several characteristics indicate that a number of components may be attractive production propositions to developing countries. The simpler items permit companies at relatively lower technological levels to compete; fixed investment costs are frequently lower than for vehicle manufacture; labor content for many components is a significant cost factor, thereby enhancing prospects in lower wage locations; transport costs relative to value in simpler components for example, wire harnesses are lower than for CBU; and barriers to entry and to product distribution tend to be fewer, above all in replacement markets.

- International trade in components is substantial. U.S. imports for the mid 1990s are in the range of $25-30 billion, of which about 20 percent come from developing countries. Though the dominance of Brazil, Mexico and Republic of Korea is again marked, some of the other selected countries have a significant presence (Thailand, Indonesia, India and Philippines). EC imports of components from developing countries overwhelm purchases of vehicles, and are estimated at about $4 billion for the mid 1990s. Sources are quite diversified; indeed, it is the region in closest proximity (Eastern Europe) which is lagging though exports should grow as some of the engine plants enter larger scale production.

- Trade in components among developing countries exceeds $1 billion. It is regionally focussed and suggests that cost savings for vehicle assembly could be achieved if, for example, "regional content" were accepted instead of local content in domestic manufacturing policies of the larger developing countries.

- Restructuring of the component sector receives less publicity than that of assembly but is every bit as urgent (and necessary!) on an international scale. Standards of quality, cost and just-in-time (JIT) delivery, coupled with moves by assemblers towards global out-sourcing and single-sourcing, are altering the structure of the component industry, accentuating its stratification into top tier firms (design capabilities) and others functioning at less sophisticated levels. Some of the top component firms are now coming to rival the assemblers in capabilities, outstrip them in profitability, and be better placed as regards vulnerability. If the VW drive towards "logistical suppliers," already practiced to an extent by some assemblers, is broadly replicated by other vehicle producers, then the leading component companies are likely to assemble whole segments of vehicles and deliver the resulting modules to the vehicle producers.

- The upper echelons among the component companies are now global, which implies a strong interest in foreign direct investment opportunities. Appropriate policies by developing countries, including encouragement of joint ventures and alliances, can give these countries a good position to attract investment, for export as well as domestic markets.

Organizational Imperatives

Automotive companies, assemblers as well as suppliers, are faced with new challenges relating to quality standards regardless of location. They need to respond to these challenges by adopting strategies based on the optimization of assets they have access to, relative to the markets they will serve in the future.

Standards Which Companies Must Meet

Since the mid 1980s the automotive industry has been characterized not so much by globalization reckoned in terms of trade and investment but by the globalization of corporate attitudes. Those attitudes crystallize around a set of standards, for products and processes, which all firms hoping to survive and prosper in the automotive industry must strive to attain and enhance. The standards put the accent on quality in three dimensions. In relation to the vehicle user the key characteristics are safety, comfort and adaptability, and environmental soundness. Vis-a-vis the distributor, the maintenance of brief delivery times and full service are essential. Within the production system, major changes are in-plant, with the accent on individual worker polyvalence, team solutions to problems, the weakening of hierarchies and, above all, the detection and elimination of difficulties before they affect production - quality is built in and zero defect becomes the norm. But the impact on component producers is likewise enormous. In day-to-day production they must maintain product standards and quick schedules (inventory

10

minimization), while their participation in design (at least for first tier component companies) becomes a crucial aspect of gaining and retaining business.

It would be a fundamental error in policy thinking and company planning for developing countries to suppose that the standards just described do not apply to them. While these markets are still partly separated from the OECD, the forces impelling them towards global best practice are powerful:

- Vehicle exports, even if they are of lower priced models, must compete against products manufactured in the OECD. Where the standards referred to here have been translated into legislation (which is the case for safety and environment), the quality factor is a necessary condition for exports. Where they have not, the awareness of buyers is sufficient to ensure that quality will be crucial in their purchase decisions.

- To the extent that emerging markets gradually permit more CBU imports, these will set higher quality standards in domestic markets and thereby force local producers to meet the international norms.

- In every one of the selected countries, multinational corporations hold total or partial control over the assembly firms. It would follow, therefore, that foreign direct investment, whether in new plant or renovation/restructuring of old, will be aimed at meeting the multinational corporations overall standards (image matters in all markets) while plant reorganization also moves in the same direction. Mexican companies where U.S. multinational corporations hold strong interests have recently been at the top of the global benchmarking exercises conducted by the parent firms. In such instances the real labor cost advantage of developing countries exceeds their wage differential advantage, due to the additional productivity edge.

- Component manufacture, especially original equipment manufacture, is driven by the assembly requirements. Once again, the wave of component foreign direct investment in several of the selected countries conforms to the international norms. Furthermore, to the extent that the countries want to raise local content, export vehicles, and encourage foreign direct investment, they will have to upgrade quality in components. The automotive industry world of the next few years will not be one for half measures.

Optimization of Assets

The spread of global best practice, the increase of design and investment cost for products whose life cycles (measured across many markets as well as within individual ones) have become shorter, the severe reduction in growth in major markets, and the persistence of the "management of markets mentality", have forced even the world's largest automotive industry firms to optimize on the assets they possess and use them to obtain usufruct of assets they do not own and/or control. Negotiations to create new, profitable asset combinations has been and will remain an organizational imperative - its impact on automotive operations in United States/Europe/Asia is summarized in Chart 1.

Corporate assets which enter such deals depend mainly (though not solely) on genuine capabilities for example, command over a given technology. Sometimes "positional" factors that is, directly related to a particular market, can also be influenced by a firm - an obvious instance is where an individual company can affect protectionist policy of the government. A country's assets are almost entirely of the positional type - straight geographic location, availability of low wage labor, control over government

11

policy. Whether the asset be of the capability or the position type, however, its value is always subject to erosion.

Both automotive industry companies and emerging market governments are frequently caught off balance in face of shifting asset values. For example, it appears that VW's quality image cannot sustain its cost structure, nor its proximity to Central Europe is necessarily a guarantee of success in major new investment programs; Ford's network strength in Western Europe has not been enough to protect market shares with the advent of the single market (even though that market is far from unified); Brazil cannot

CHART 1

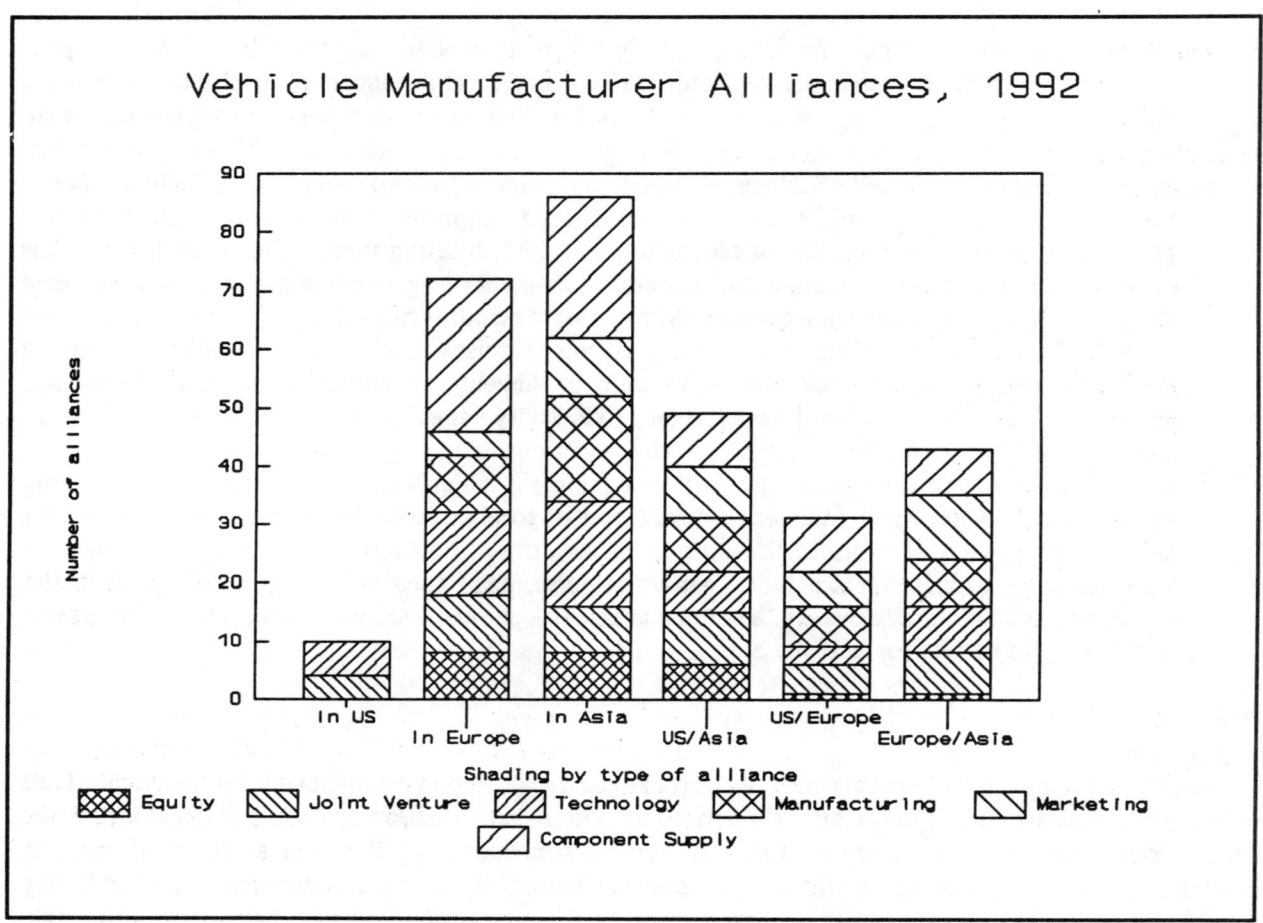

Note: Asia = Japan and Korea.
Source: *Wards Automotive Handbook.* 1992.

rely solely on its size to attract foreign direct investment or its labor costs to promote exports, as its long running export promotion program, BEFIEX, has competitors in several countries which are also attractive as production locations. Thailand has been in the investment limelight since at least the start

12

of the 1990s and highly optimistic forecasts of its automotive industry future are regularly offered. As long as rapid economic growth persists, the country should remain favored. However, policy changes towards modernization of market structure, particularly to permit larger scale output by individual firms, would reinforce its status.

The central challenge governments in the emerging countries must confront is: how can they maximize use of positional assets they possess to encourage companies to locate top capability production there? Only since the late 1980s have some of the governments stopped thinking in terms of their control space that is, the areas of automotive industry activity over which they can exercise policy command. Yet the idea that the decision space which they can influence is ample has still not taken hold. One of the purposes of the many-sided policy dialogue IFC is promoting is precisely to raise awareness of this possibility.

Strategic Positioning

Policy for the automotive industry must be framed against the market positioning choices which the leading vehicle assemblers have made and/or might be persuaded to make. Chart 2 shows the assembly position in the early/mid 1990s and suggests the following observations:

- The matrix shows some regional concentration, although this is weakening over time. The Japanese companies are in Asia, while US and European companies are in South America. Only in Central Europe is there some mix, with VW, Fiat, Suzuki and GM.

- By major company some geographic separation is evident. Toyota focusses on ASEAN as a production site, GM and Ford on the principal Latin American countries, VW or Latin America and Czech Republic. Most producers, however, have become active in China.

- Suzuki is the one firm using developing country locations distant from each other.

- Since competition in these markets is now quite strong, and the financial state of most of the leading firms is difficult, it seems improbable that there will be much change in the form of the matrix over the next few years.

The message is clear: governments should concentrate in the short run on improving the environment for those multinational corporations (and their local partners) already manufacturing domestically. Only in the medium term are efforts aimed at potential new entrants likely to yield much return. Clarity of the message, unfortunately, does not mean that its implementation is simple. Policies designed to raise efficiency through modifying market structure can affect the survival of existing producers; policies relaxing local content requirements in return for greater exports can offer larger potential advantages to some rather than others; all assembly firms might be suffering from weaknesses in domestic component production which could be tackled through greater foreign direct investment but in components.

The implication is that only with access to considerable technical and communication skills, a good deal of market specific information, and substantial dialogue, can the policies work. The transition of the 1990s requires a qualitatively superior policy effort.

CHART 2

MAIN CORPORATE MANUFACTURING/ASSEMBLY ACTIVITY OF MNC IN "NEW" GROWTH COUNTRIES, EARLY 1990s

COUNTRY/COMPANY	TOYOTA	NISSAN	HONDA	MAZDA	MITSUBISHI	SUZUKI	GM	FORD	VW	FIAT	RENAULT	CHRYSLER	PEUGEOT
CHINA							◉		◉				◉
INDONESIA	◉		◉	◉	◉	◉							
MALAYSIA	◉				◉								
THAILAND	◉	◉	◉	◉	◉								
REPUBLIC OF KOREA				◉	◉		◉	◉					
TAIWAN, CHINA		◉						◉					
MEXICO		◉										◉	
BRAZIL							◉	◉	◉	◉			
VENEZUELA							◉	◉		◉			
CZECH & SLOVAK FEDERAL REPUBLIC									◉				
HUNGARY						◉							
POLAND							◉	◉		◉			
TURKEY	◉						◉				◉		
ARGENTINA								◉	◉	◉	◉		◉

Source: "A Report on the Automotive Industry Seminar Held in Jakarta, Indonesia". IFC, May 1991.

III. *Structure of the Automotive Industry in Selected Countries*

The Assembly Industry

In the preceding section, Table 2 showed the extent of production in the selected countries while Chart 2 complemented this with a map of multinational corporation presence. The purpose of this sub-section is to examine further the size, structure and content of output; a crucial dimension of the policy debate is the way in which those elements can be improved, especially in passenger cars.

Table 4 synthesizes the information on market structure by firm. Read in conjunction with Table 2 data on output, the figures suggest that the two Andean and three ASEAN countries are the ones suffering from diseconomies of scale that is, even the leading firms cannot generate sufficient volume to keep down unit costs. The conclusion is reinforced by the plethora of models sold, many of which do not have interchangeable parts. Consumer prices are thus higher than larger scale manufacture would allow while those components made at home likewise cannot reap scale benefits unless export markets can be gained. In comparison with the mid 1980s there has been greater concentration in Brazil/Argentina (due to the fusion of Ford and VW into Autolatina) but some weakening in the Asean countries. Unfortunately domestic demand has been volatile with no overall tendency to grow in South America so that firms there cannot readily count on larger scale production.

Economic inefficiency, however, does not necessarily imply lack of profitability for individual firms. The data on this key point are not particularly reliable nor easy to interpret. Certainly financial results have varied sharply from year to year in Latin America, have been on the whole good in the Pacific Rim, and poor in Central Europe (where the very concepts of corporate financial management have only recently begun to be used). Companies have been able to stay in business, or even prosper, for a variety of reasons external to the economics of the automotive industry in the country where they operate. Those reasons include the high prices (particularly of passenger cars) which the markets have borne; transfer pricing operations available to firms where multinational corporations have a significant stake and the volume of intra-trade is large; in some cases, the availability of credit at low or negative real rates of interest; and dealings by the firms in activities bearing little or no relation to the automotive industry.

All of this may be a valuable cushion in conditions of virtually permanent and pronounced uncertainty. But the fact is that companies will only strengthen their real performance if they are able to focus management energy on the competitiveness problems. Policy, not just to the automotive industry itself but for the economy as a whole, must maximize that space (see Section IV below).

The Component Industry

Production and trade characteristics of components are summarized in Table 5 (data for Central Europe are not included due to unreliability). In this disparate picture the main features are:

- Firm size varies enormously within and across countries, with Brazil/Argentina appearing relatively the strongest of the selected countries.

- Foreign ties are important to the bigger companies, especially through licensing agreements.

15

TABLE 4

STRUCTURE OF ASSEMBLY INDUSTRY IN SELECTED COUNTRIES, EARLY 1990s, COMPARED WITH MID 1980s

REGION/COUNTRY	MID 1980s		1990s	
	No. of firms	Output Share of Top 3 (percent)	No. of firms	Output Share of Top 3 (percent)
I. AMERICAS				
Mexico	5	68	5	66
Brazil	7	82	5	95
Argentina	4	82	3	100
Colombia	3	100	3	100
Venezuela	6	76	7	70
II. PACIFIC RIM				
Republic of Korea	3	100	6	95
Taiwan, China	10	40	10	48
Indonesia	12	64	12	54
Malaysia	7	75	7	62
Thailand	8	70	8	66
III. CENTRAL EUROPE				
Czech Republic	1	100	1	100
Hungary	-	--	2	100
Poland	2	100	2	100
IV. INDIVIDUAL COUNTRIES				
India	5	75	5	88
China	13	46	18	48

Source: Authors' calculations.

TABLE 5

CHARACTERISTICS OF THE COMPONENT SECTOR IN SELECTED COUNTRIES, MID 1990s

REGION/COUNTRY	No. of Firms	PRODUCTION CHARACTERISTICS			FOREIGN TIES	
		Size Distribution	Turnover ($bn.)	OEM/RM Split	Equity/Control	Exports
I. AMERICAS						
Mexico	500	About 25 percent of firms employ ≥ 1000	6	40/60	Many joint ventures	20-25 percent of turnover
Brazil	550	About 14 percent of firms employ ≥ 1000	15	50/50	20 percent of all firms are foreign affiliates, mainly the largest companies. Many licensing agreements	15-20 percent of turnover
Argentina	600	About 20 percent employ > 400	2	25/75	15 percent of firms are affiliates; many licensing agreements	10-15 percent of turnover
Colombia	200	9 percent of firms account for 60 percent sales	0.25	N/A	Minimal equity: many licenses	3 percent of turnover
Venezuela	200	30 percent of firms employ > 100	0.8	20/80	Equity now permitted: licensing	12 percent of turnover
II. PACIFIC RIM						
Republic of Korea	1100	5 percent employ > 1000	12	80/20	Many licensing agreements	10 percent of turnover
Taiwan, China	250/300	N/A	5	50/50	60 percent of firms have Japanese links	20 percent of turnover
Indonesia	200	N/A	4	N/A	Many licensing agreements	5-10 percent of turnover
Malaysia	200	N/A	1	40/60	Limited	Negligible
Thailand	350	N/A	4	40/60	N/A	5-10 percent of turnover

Source: Authors' calculations.

- Total turnover across countries shows a much larger spread than for the assembly business.

- Original equipment manufacture share of output is bigger, the larger is vehicle output.

- All countries export some of their output, with shares up to 20 percent.

The product mix is wide and influenced powerfully by technology levels and local content legislation, which frequently provides full or partial protection to domestic manufacturers of specified major items. Though the barriers to entry are fairly low, and domestic competition can be quite strong, the involvement of foreign firms is not too widespread but seems to be necessary if constant improvements in cost and quality are to be made.

Neither in components nor assembly do the selected countries possess technology of their own, even if considerable learning by doing has taken place. To meet international standards, technology imports will be needed and this will lead to rationalization of the component sector (even more so if local content is to be raised without sacrificing quality). The task here will be still greater than assembly and require more wide-ranging policies.

Domestic Demand

The composition of vehicle sales varies widely across countries, as Table 6 demonstrates. In Asia particularly (Indonesia, China, Thailand) the passenger car share is one-quarter or less while in Central Europe along with Brazil and Argentina it reaches three-quarters or more. While there is obviously demand for heavy commercial vehicles in all countries, the pivot on which the passenger car share swings is the behavior of demand for light commercial vehicles. Indonesia and Thailand especially use them as multi-purpose transport; in Indonesia there is even a further development, in that the bodies and seating of light commercial vehicles are frequently converted to render them more suitable for passenger transport. Conversion is done by so-called "carroserie" builders of whom there are about 215 in the country. This fact alone strongly suggests the existence of a substantial latent demand for straight passenger cars. If price structures, which are the outcome of government production licensing and tax policies, were allowed to change directly through the market instead of indirectly, there could be an appreciable rise in the passenger car share.

There are, all the same, good reasons why future policymaking in South American and Asian countries should examine carefully the possibilities in the light/medium commercial vehicles branch of the automotive industry. First, though urbanization is increasing in all countries, the need for vehicles which can withstand long journeys over tough terrain and poor roads is indeed great. Second, low incomes plus the necessity of maximizing household/business use of a vehicle, indicate that light commercial vehicles will retain their appeal. Third, multinational corporations are devoting much greater attention in new model design to the light commercial vehicle sector. There might be opportunities to bring these items very quickly onto developing country markets, where known demand is available, rather than incur the heavy promotional cost of creating/encouraging demand in OECD locations.

The first section of the study underlined how development of the automotive industry in developing countries has responded to a perverse philosophy, in that countries have wanted domestic production yet constantly kept control over domestic demand. Why? Because the automotive industry has in essence been regarded, and in many instances still is regarded, as a producer good rather than a consumer good. In other words, countries have stimulated output because of linkage effects with the rest

18

of the industrial production system. Certainly the foreign exchange angle has always mattered, usually through import substitution and occasionally through exports. But the encouragement of domestic demand has been thought of as inimical to these aims rather than as supportive of them.

It would be interesting to see whether this central bias of policy will alter in the next few years. Proponents of this change argue that impetus to output expansion is far more likely to come from internal rather than external sales, and that the introduction of new products and processes, as well as restructuring in the industrial sector, can be managed much better in a growth scenario than in one of stagnation. In this light, production increases should be promoted by greater home demand instead of being negated by restrained demand.

TABLE 6

SHARE OF PASSENGER CARS IN TOTAL VEHICLE SALES, SELECTED COUNTRIES, 1991 (percent)

REGION/COUNTRY	PASSENGER CAR SHARE (percent)
I. AMERICAS	
Mexico	61
Brazil	75
Argentina	82
Colombia	62
Venezuela	48
II. PACIFIC RIM	
Republic of Korea	68
Taiwan, China	72
Indonesia	16
Malaysia	63
Thailand	25
III. CENTRAL EUROPE	
Czech Republic	87
Hungary	73
Poland	93
IV. INDIVIDUAL COUNTRIES	
India	60
China	15

Source: *1992 Market Data Book*, New York, 1992.

How has internal demand been restrained? Besides import taxes and duties, the principal policy instrument has been direct taxation of sales, mainly through excise duties and purchase taxes. In most of the selected countries the percentage rates have reached 50 percent and in some substantially more of ex-factory costs, these costs themselves being high relative to OECD levels. The official prices, however, are not an accurate guide to the real demand position since physical shortage of vehicles (cars) has been the norm in many places. Black markets have flourished, with side payments to jump the queue a common feature. The chronic absence of credit facilities has contributed to narrowing of the potential customer base and thereby consolidated an image of the car as an item affordable only for a small elite - not the image that many developing countries wanted to project. Running costs, especially petroleum prices, are not a handicap (several of the selected developing countries are significant petroleum producers) but in some instances insurance charges are exceptionally large (itself a reflection of high replacement cost of damaged vehicles).

Automotive Trade

The leading developing countries were, until the present decade, concerned with two issues in trade: control over vehicle imports, and export promotion of CBU vehicles and engines. Table 3 indicates how policies for the former have fared. In value terms, Brazil manages CBU external sales of around $1 billion which, while still much below the yardstick locations of Mexico (> $2 billion) and Republic of Korea (around $5 billion), does give a strong boost to the balance of trade. Engine exports have begun to reach significant levels in Brazil ($0.2 billion) and are starting in Thailand and Hungary. Nevertheless, it appears that the critical trade changes in this decade will stem from components.

Modernization requires major improvement to product and this can only be achieved when components and subsystems of requisite quality are used. The numerical translation of this is vivid in the yardstick countries. Since the late 1980s, when modernization gathered pace, Mexico's balance of trade in components has registered a growing deficit which alone has turned the automotive industry balance negative. Given that Mexico exports a sizeable volume of smaller components (witness the burgeoning of maquiladora trade), besides engine sales of about $1.5 billion per annum, the surge of component imports has indeed been strong. Republic of Korea, for its part, has about 30 percent Japanese content in its vehicles, again the consequence of component imports.

The selected countries already have appreciable deficits in the component trade balance. Although some exports could be made in the next years, these countries will need to import most of the major components necessary for restructuring. Those components must either be imported directly, or the technology necessary for their production locally must be imported. Foreign exchange outflow will show up either in the automotive trade balance or in royalty/license payments. Policy must start from the premise that a significant and lasting improvement of automotive industry performance, and in particular an effort at reaching international standards, is certain to worsen the component balance for quite some years. The objective of policy should be to ensure that the deterioration is a worthwhile investment, in the sense that local production capabilities are genuinely strengthened and, if possible, that subsequent export opportunities are created. In this perspective trade issues might best be dealt with through policies aimed at investment and technology rather than at trade as such.

Measuring Rods of Investment and Production for Developing Countries

The information presented above and the analysis of policy which is the substance of Section IV can be linked together via the core facts governing automotive industry investment and output. Figures refer to passenger car economics; some minor modifications are in order for commercial vehicles. Chart 3 synthesizes the investment costs, optimum scale range and labor content for the four main stages of production.

CHART 3

MAJOR ECONOMIC CHARACTERISTICS BY STAGE (AUTOMOTIVE)

STAGE	INVESTMENT LEVEL	SCALE	LABOR CONTENT	LOGISTICS/TRANSPORT COSTS
Assembly	$400-500 million	100 to 200,000	More than 50 percent	10 percent
Major component	$400-500 million	500,000	10-20 percent	5-15 percent
Moderate processed parts/systems	$50-200 million	500,000 to 1,000,000	10-20 percent	5-15 percent
rough process parts/systems	$20-100 million	200,000 to 1,000,000	10-20 percent Except wiring harness, trim. radio assembly 30 percent or more	5-15 percent Higher for some plastic. Lower for electronics

Source: IFC Data.

Assembly has relatively the lowest scale, the highest labor content, and (provided a 100,000 volume is attained) offers a cost edge of at least 30 percent compared with OECD assembly. But assembly is quite a small share of total car cost and the penalties for sub-optimal scale are severe - so the advantages from local assembly are relatively much less significant than is usually implied (Chart 4).

CHART 4

PASSENGER CAR ASSEMBLY ECONOMICS: DEVELOPING VERSUS DEVELOPED COUNTRY

	DEVELOPING (E.G. BRAZIL)	DEVELOPED
Volume per year	100,000	200,000
Per unit labor hours (total)	48	22-30
Wage rate (with fringe)	3-5	20-30
Per unit labor costs	144-240	440-900
Per unit other costs (depreciation, taxes, utilities, overhead)	450	500-600
TOTAL ASSEMBLY COST	594-690	940-1500

Source: IFC Data.

Component manufacture (the bottom two rows of Chart 3) covers a range of products some of which do lend themselves to very large scale operations with fairly high labor content and low labor costs that is, are prime candidates for global/ regional sourcing from developing countries. Opportunities for such items have been taken up in regional centers for example, Mexico.

The ability to translate the assembly cost edge into a genuine market advantage is dependent upon the quality of components used and the quality of assembly itself. The latter is a function of plant organization and labor skill, whereas the former reverts back to the points made earlier regarding the role of components. Unless components are fully competitive, the assembly advantage will be nullified.

CHART 5

COMPONENTS OF CAR COST

- Assembly   15 percent

- Body and body parts   25 percent

- Engine/transmission   25 percent
- Final drive/suspension/steering/brakes

                                                                    15 percent

- Other   20 percent

Source: IFC Data.

Many original-equipment-manufacture components do not have a particularly favorable economic structure for developing countries production and they do absorb a large share of total vehicle cost (see Chart 5). The selected countries all have big internal markets supplied almost entirely from domestic bases - if policy could encourage improved efficiency of manufacture of these components (for example, through free trade areas to reap economies of scale), the economic and commercial profitability would almost certainly be substantial.

IV. *Policy Performance and Policy Prospects*

The Policy Process and Its Participants

A realistic assessment of policy behavior towards the automotive industry needs some understanding of who becomes involved, what kinds of policies and/or decisions are taken, and the degree to which they are implemented. Transparency, stability and applicability are criteria that ideally might be employed, yet nowhere in the world would the policy process score high marks on those indicators. More relevant is the extent to which the process gives producers, in particular, enough confidence to carry out investment/modernization programs. Two preliminary points have to be made clear. First, this subsection considers only policies directly aimed at the automotive industry - the impacts of macroeconomic management are dealt with in the next subsection. Second, Central European countries are in a radically different situation than other regions. The January 1993 division of Czech Republic into two separate states, added to the breakup of previous regimes elsewhere in Central and Eastern Europe, means that a totally new policymaking process is under creation. One of the risks of the new situation is to suppose that nothing should be done. This report argues that, on the contrary, specific actions are required and that experiences in other countries can provide a guide.

The key participants in policymaking in the selected countries are certain government offices and ministries; business associations and on occasion individual businessmen; and foreign groups, including (depending on the policy) automotive firms, trade lobbies and financial entities. In specifics, the ministries most frequently concerned, that is, those dealing with industry and with trade, are at the center of the debate over market structure regulations and local content. Typically the Industry Ministry is often heavily immersed in issues of ownership and foreign investment legislation/implementation. But the strategic significance of the automotive industry virtually guarantees involvement of the Ministry of Economics and/or Finance, in some cases a Planning Board, and on sensitive matters the President's (or Prime Minister's) office. Generalizations about the attitudes of these entities and the influence each of them exercises are tricky, especially in the mid 1990s phase of transition. Subject to that caveat, industry ministries tend to be the most ardent supporters of greater local content and tougher restrictions on foreign ownership/control. On market structure policies they have frequently been ambivalent, especially when conflicting interests among domestic producers have been at stake. Significant shifts in structures have tended to occur under the initiative of groups other than the Industry Ministry.

Trade ministries see their role in essence as that of securing the best possible foreign exchange position - their bias is towards import control but they often show a readiness to innovate with regard to export promotion (including compensating trade arrangements). In the South American countries they are active in support of sub-regional accords in the automotive industry. To an increasing extent in all selected countries, the promotional dimensions of policy need support functions for example, trade fairs for components, exploratory missions abroad to seek out joint venture partners and training of export promotion specialists. There are some signs for example, in Argentina and Thailand, of programs jointly conceived and operated by trade ministries and business associations.

The Economics/Finance ministry has the single most powerful impact on demand, through fiscal and credit policies. Early 1990s trends have been towards some relaxation of fiscal pressures (for example, the February 1993 tax cuts on smaller-engine vehicles in Brazil) on the argument that demand for automobiles has a high price elasticity so that total fiscal revenues rise if percentage charges per unit are reduced. In the case of latent demand, income elasticity is high so that even with high sales taxes demand remains strong, as was the situation in Brazil in the early sixties and in Central and Eastern Europe with the liberalization of imports. Moves to assist the creation of more efficient and broader credit markets have also begun to offer some stimuli to would-be vehicle buyers, especially in the ASEAN countries.

Automotive industry business associations in the selected countries share a number of characteristics:

- In nearly all cases assemblers are more effectively organized than component manufacturers. If associations of the latter do exist, their political influence is minimal.

- Membership includes strong participation of multinational corporations through their local affiliates.

- They have tended to function more as spokesmen for assemblers vis-a-vis government ministries (sometimes perceived as adversaries) rather than as entities oriented towards provision of industrial services to their members.

Given the way the automotive industry has developed in most developing countries those features are not surprising; their policy implications nevertheless merit enumeration. First, the associations tend to behave as one in discussions on policy changes affecting overall demand and mandatory local content requirements - in both instances the pressure is on the relevant ministries to relax restrictions. Second, on all policies which are liable to alter appreciably the structure of the assembly market, the internal strains are usually severe. Multinational corporation attitudes are increasingly influenced by strategic requirements at headquarters while local managers do not want to risk market share. Third, the same considerations tend to mean ambivalence towards regional trade promotion agreements - the cripplingly slow progress among ASEAN countries is a telling example. At one time or another, Ford, Mitsubishi and Toyota have each proposed their own schemes for integration, yet have reportedly thwarted any ventures that would bring about widespread rationalization. Fourth, the effect of assembly-side policies on local component production does not receive sufficient attention from business interests since parts manufacturers themselves rarely have a strong voice in the proceedings.

The kinds of decisions made, or the styles of automotive industry policymaking in Asia and South America, can be characterized as follows:

- In South America, the promulgation (very frequent in the early 1990s) of wide-ranging decrees which set out the "automotive industry policy". This approach tends to push aside smoother, more gradual adjustments which might ultimately have greater impact.

- Protracted negotiations prior to decree publication, often giving the impression of continuous argument but little useful dialogue.

- In Asia the acrimonious exchanges are just as prevalent but they do not often result in much policy change at all.

- The atmosphere in both regions is thus of ever-present possibilities of legislative change, requiring significant expenditure of lobbying resources by firms.

24

- The occurrence from time to time of major decisions, normally involving a new entrant to the assembly market, which tend to come through the President/Prime Minister's office and provide "shocks to the system". These decisions escape the policy frames just mentioned (the 1993 import liberalization in Brazil is a case in point).

In none of the selected countries is the policymaking process smooth. It is marked by a constant tug-of-war not only between government ministries and business associations but also within each group; the resultant movement is usually disproportionately small compared to the effort expended. For many of the participants, maintenance of the legislative status quo is probably the real objective.

This frustrating state of affairs is compounded by severe difficulties of policy implementation. Governments tend to overestimate their control space in two crucial dimensions. Relative to the details of policy, they give excessive weight to administrative capabilities and not enough to possibilities firms possess to elude the requirements. Relative to the speed and type of change dictated by the market, they set policy too rigidly - changes of gear are then made in jerky fashion. The outcome is a weakening of confidence in the whole process, and possibly less investment than might otherwise be made.

Policies on Automotive Production

These policies relate to ownership, licensing of production and local content regulations. In all three areas the trend is for increased liberalization although local content presents a mixed picture as some Asian countries have opted for rather tight controls.

Ownership of Firms

Two dimensions of ownership policies/decisions are important: the public/private split, and the domestic/foreign division. On the former, state participation in equity now exists only in a few assembly companies viz. Maruti in India, Proton in Malaysia, the joint ventures with VW, Peugeot, Chrysler and GM in China, joint ventures with Fiat and GM in Poland, and small shareholdings of governments in some other companies in various places. South American governments have removed themselves entirely from the production sphere. In no instance, apart from China, is any share capital of component firms held by public authorities. By and large the mid 1990s situation corresponds well to the conditions of each country - multinational corporations would be unlikely to have significant involvement in China unless the government were also seen to be present, while similar implicit guarantees have a value in Poland. Conditions will alter, however, and State equity holdings will most likely continue to decline.

Driven by the need to encourage foreign exchange inflows and the recognition that the automotive industry required modernization and restructuring, a number of the selected countries have liberalized policies in recent years. The main policy trends and their impacts are:

- In South America the assemblers are wholly or majority owned by multinational corporations. There are no restrictions on entry to component production either and this is reflected in the stakes taken in leading firms, which are usually foreign affiliates.

- Central Europe has yet to attract notable component foreign direct investment but the assembly sector (cars) is now undergoing major transformation thanks to VW in the Czech Republic, Suzuki in Hungary, and Fiat and GM in Poland. Engine plants to supply W. Europe are, however, on the increase.

25

- The Asian countries remain those where foreign equity holdings, though present in nearly all assembly firms and in the larger component enterprises, rarely reach a majority stake (though control is often assured via other well-known mechanisms). In several countries formal legislative instruments limit share-holding (the three giants of China, India, and Indonesia are the outstanding cases) and in others, implicit government policies (for example, statements of intentions, preferences) encourage corporate prudence and thus restrain foreign equity. But it is precisely in Asia where technology licensing (often tied to minority foreign equity) occurs most frequently.

From these observations a quite clearly defined picture of ownership policies and trends in the automotive industry appears. South America and Central Europe are the regions where macroeconomic policy changes have been most striking, and where the desire to promote capital inflows and modernize has been greatest. This will in all probability persist, especially as in South America more countries try to link together via sub-regional arrangements. Success, as measured by the results these external ties bring, will be shaped by the quality of the investments and the degree of upgrading they can bring. United States and European firms, both in South America and Central Europe, should likely be the prime movers.

Asian countries, contrary to the impression often given because of their extensive involvement in the trading system, retain much more protectionist policies. Domestic groups keep majority holdings in assembly and component plants, in most instances with Japanese partners who also supply technology. With everyone determined to keep out vehicle imports, and each Japanese partner not wishing to lose ground against others from Japan, the assembly operations continue to be high cost. The sustainability of this structure is doubtful. Its persistence depends on sustained expansion of domestic vehicle demand (CBU exports from the selected Asian countries are not a likely short-term prospect) and/or the maintenance of relatively high profit margins per unit. Paradoxical though it may seem, South American countries might be better placed in the modernization drive.

Licensing of Production

In this policy dimension also, the South American and Central European countries now operate open policies in assembly whereas the Asian countries retain constraints. Controls over entry of new companies are severe in all Asian selected countries. Production allocation is still frequently practiced through devices such as limiting the firms permitted to manufacture certain categories of vehicle and juggling fiscal systems to encourage sales of those categories in preference to others. This kind of market management can work if economic growth shelters too many producers from harsh suffering - but any slowdowns in Asia will place existing policies under scrutiny.

Local Content Practices

No set of policies has been so contentious in the automotive industry as that relating to local content. It is here that the objectives of encouraging domestic industrialization, controlling imports, and controlling cost and quality, join together and come into conflict. Table 7 synthesizes the mid 1990s position in Latin America and Asia, with the "yardstick" countries included and information given for both cars and commercial vehicles. Several key policy trends are highlighted by the table:

- The tendency since the beginning of the 1990s has been for South American producers to reduce mandatory minimum local content levels and to permit more flexibility in meeting the levels set.

26

In every case the mid 1990s legislation provides much wider import opportunities than was previously the case.

● The Asian countries have not followed the same pattern. In part this is because the rates in some countries were below those in South America, and in part because they wanted to avoid too heavy an outflow of foreign exchange.

TABLE 7

LOCAL CONTENT REGULATIONS IN SELECTED COUNTRIES, 1993

REGION/COUNTRY	MINIMUM LOCAL CONTENT REQUIRED (percent)			OTHER DETAILS
	Passenger Cars	Light CV	Heavy CV	
I. AMERICAS				
Mexico	36	36	36	Policy since December 1989; rate computed as average across a manufacturer's entire product range.
Brazil	70/75	70/75	70/75	Since 1991; compliance needed to be eligible for subsidized financing from National Development Bank.
Argentina	40	42	42	Until 31/12/94; from 1995 until 31 December 1999 levels will be decided by Mercosur agreements. Vehicle exports which wish to qualify for import rights must contain 25 percent local content stemming from the nationally owned parts producers.
Colombia	--	--	--	Positive lists exist for items to be produced domestically: debate on switching to a percent rate formula in which labor costs would be excluded.
Venezuela	--	--	--	Decree 1335 of 11 December 1990 replaced LC rules with a minimum forex earnings requirement which includes allowance for incorporation of local parts as well as exports.

Source: "A Report on the Automotive Industry Seminar Held in Jakarta, Indonesia". IFC, May 1991.

● Brazil continues (despite reducing mandatory requirements) to have a far more "national based" automotive industry than any other country. The breadth and depth of its component sector were illustrated earlier in the report; if it can amplify some of its automotive industry policies still further, then (macroeconomic conditions permitting) it can modernize from an industrial system which many would argue is qualitatively and quantitatively stronger than that in any other of the selected countries.

- No one is likely to make dramatic shifts in local content policy in the medium term. Greater foreign direct investment in the component sector can bring about upgrading and reduce the cost penalty for local manufacture.

The data in Table 7, when analyzed alongside some of the other policy trends already surveyed, reinforce the conclusion that the South American countries are moving quite far in the direction of greater efficiency and that, whatever else the Asian producers may have accomplished, they are still some way both from the existing automotive industry capabilities in Brazil and Argentina and from putting together coherent sets of policies which would give a strong push along the road.

Macroeconomic Policies and Automotive Development

The differential performance of the selected countries in recent years has owed more to macroeconomic policy differences than to any other single factor. The ASEAN countries, especially Thailand, enjoyed fast growth under stable macroeconomic policies; China, a period of enormous expansion; South American countries had to survive falling per capita incomes as well as violent swings in economic activity; the Central European countries stagnated prior to complete system collapse; and India experienced a dramatic deterioration in its debt situation, followed by liberalization.

The cost to the countries of past macroeconomic policy failures have been so great and so visible that a much sounder economic framework in the next few years is now recognized as a necessary condition of improved performance. The changes completed (or in progress) and which should yield most for the automotive industry are:

- Exchange rates that reflect the underlying production conditions and move more or less in accordance with spreads in inflation rates across countries.

- Rates of inflation in many countries are far lower than in previous years and which permit business plans to be formulated with a reasonable chance that estimates for main parameters are accurate.

- Liberalization of price structures, again permitting production and purchase decisions to be made freely and the underlying profitability of various activities and locations to be properly compared.

- Much greater flexibility in labor markets, allowing productivity improvements based on better plant organization and enhanced techniques (physical equipment).

- Privatization of companies with strong input/output links to the automotive industry firms, and increased competition in the markets for those products. This change is a key move towards system efficiency in the automotive industry.

- Reductions in overall levels of protection (and not just in the automotive industry) allowing cheaper production and some further export possibilities.

28

- A pronounced liberalization of foreign direct investment regimes, technology licensing regulations and other legislation influencing the import of assets critical to programs of industrial modernization.

The extent and pace of the changes, as well as their actual/probable impacts, obviously differ widely among the selected countries. But by far their most important feature is the message they convey. Just as corporate management is seized with the recognition that global best practice sets the tone for performance, so the macroeconomic policy revolution makes it clear under which kind of market conditions the business will have to operate. In fact, attainment of global best practice at plant and company level would be impossible without greater efficiency in market operations. The relaxation of restrictions has started to occur, although at an uneven pace amongst the selected countries, at precisely the time when the quantity of information along with the electronic capacity to process it has expanded enormously. As a result it would appear that the conditions for efficiency improvement in the automotive industry of the selected countries are now beginning to come into place. Provided the macroeconomic changes continue to be pursued, the accent can switch to the central features of automotive industry policy as such.

Trade Policies

The core information on policy is given in Table 8; though the title refers to imports alone, the material presented includes the compensating trade arrangements devised in Mexico, Brazil, and Argentina (similar schemes are not in use anywhere else). Principal findings are:

- The Asian countries either totally prohibit CBU imports or impose extremely high tariffs. In Latin America the pattern is to permit imports in volumes constrained by ceilings (reckoned as a percentage of domestic production) and/or by foreign exchange generated through automotive industry exports. Tariff rates on the imports that do come in have been sharply cut in the early 1990s.

- Various countries import CKD kits at rates below those used (explicitly or implicitly) on CBU.

- Parts imports generally come in at still lower rates but there are a number of restrictions covering items which are made locally.

- Brazil is the only country which explicitly exempts machinery and equipment imports from tariff charges.

- Argentina makes explicit allowance for sub-regional trade and discriminates (at least until end 1994) in favor of CBU imports from Brazil.

- Mexico has an import price monitoring program to protect against overcharging.

Once again the message is repeated; it is South America which exhibits policy dynamism through taking appreciable steps towards much freer trade. Without doubt restrictions remain (of which Mexico's ban on car imports is perhaps the most serious). Yet if compared with the substantial quantitative barriers imposed by the EC on CBU trade from non-member countries, the VER practiced by the United States, the NTB employed in Japan, and the total or nearly-total ban imposed by most Asian countries the South

American countries today are putting together a policy package which, in relative terms, is substantially more progressive.

An important feature of Table 8 is the incentive to sub-regional trade alluded to above. Analyses which stress regionalization forces in the automotive industry economy, pointing to three mega-regions and their respective developing country hinterlands, often pay little attention to whether and how developing countries organize themselves in and around the triad. Available evidence suggests that some Latin American countries, especially Mexico, have made a start toward regional integration but Asian countries generally remain noticeably divided. The hopeful signs in the Americas include: Mercosur, especially the automotive protocols signed by Brazil and Argentina; the February 1993 G3 accord of Colombia, Venezuela and Mexico; the quick schedule for creation of a free trade zone among four Andean countries that came into operation in October 1992; and the automotive agreement between Mexico and Chile of 1992. All of these keep the future progress, and possible extension, of NAFTA in view.

In comparison with Latin America, most Asian countries show a poor record and a less than promising perspective. Perhaps India and China can proceed on their own paths, their size and potential providing enough to interest others (despite the success of Maruti, the case of India is less convincing). But the ASEAN countries have certainly not been successful with their schemes, there is little sign they will be refurbished, at least not in the automotive industry, and the countries do not seem to exert that much pull on Japanese firms. There remains much scope for creative trade policy to keep abreast of changes in the power balances in the international automotive industry economy.

TABLE 8

BARRIERS TO AUTOMOTIVE IMPORTS IN SELECTED COUNTRIES, EARLY TO MID 1990s

I. AMERICAS

Mexico

ITEM	POLICY
• CBU Imports	→ limited to maximum of 20 percent of domestic production as of model year 1993
	→ imports require permission, which depends on a manufacturer having a favorable trade balance; relevant balance is 2:1 for model year 1993, 1.75:1 for model year 1994
• Parts Imports	→ subject to import duties which average approximately 10 percent
• Import Prices	→ closely monitored; if listed price exceeds international public prices for equivalent vehicles, manufacturer may lose import exclusivity rights
• Trade Surplus Rights	→ transferable among manufacturers

Brazil

ITEM POLICY

• Import Duties (percent of fob price)	1991	1992	1993	1994
CBU vehicles (except articulated trucks)	60	50	40	35
Articulated trucks	40	35	30	20
CKD kits	55	45	35	30
Ports (avg. tariff)	30	25	20	20

ITEM	POLICY
• Parts Imports	→ greater range of imports permitted
	→ Lei de informatica weakened making import of electronic components easier
• Machinery and Equipment Imports	→ since March 1991, import permitted duty free

Argentina

ITEM	POLICY
• CBU Imports by Manufacturers	→ must be compensated on 1:1 basis by exports (of any automotive product-CBU vehicle exports are calculated at a 20 percent premium), and/or by new fixed investment (30 percent of its value can be reckoned as exports)
	→ subject to a ceiling, calculated as percent of pervious year's domestic output. In 1993/94 share is 6 percent

Table 8 (continued)

→ duties on such imports are 2 percent until 31 December 1994; from then until 31 December 1999 will follow MERCOSUR rates; thereafter GATT rates

- CBU Imports by Non-manufacturers

  → models produced or imported by the manufacturers can be brought in without limit on payment of 22 percent tariff

  → other models may be imported, subject to quotas and on payment of duties

- Parts Imports

  → as long as compensated on 1:1 basis, importable on payment of 2 percent tariff

- Nature of Compensating Exports

  → must include ≥ 25 percent value from independent parts suppliers located in Argentina

  → vehicle manufacturers not located in Argentina can bring in their vehicles at 18 percent tariff provided they export parts for use in their vehicle manufactures abroad

Colombia

ITEM	POLICY

- CBU Imports

  → permitted at tariff of 50 percent as of January 1993 (down from 100 percent in January 1991)

- CKD Imports of Passenger Cars

  → tariff rates from 15 to 30 percent depending on engine size

- Other CKD Imports

  → tariffs from 45 percent for LCV to 8 percent for HCV

- Parts Imports

  → designated components cannot be imported; others pay average 30 percent duty

Venezuela

ITEM   POLICY

- Import Duties (percent) on CBU

	1991	1992	1993
Passenger cars and LCV (Engines ≤ 3000 cc)	40	30	30
Engines > 3000 cc	74	68	68
HCV	30	20	20

- Permitted CBU Imports

  → only models identical to those already assembled in Venezuela

- CKD Import Duties

  → passenger cars and LCV: 10 percent   HCV: 1 percent

- Parts Imports

  → subject to duties averaging 30 percent

Table 8 (continued)

II. PACIFIC RIM

Republic of Korea

ITEM	POLICY
● CBU Tariffs	→ tariff 25 percent
	→ acquisition duty of 2-15 percent of sales price, depending on that price
	→ excise duty of 10-25 percent depending on engine size
● Parts Tariffs	→ 15 percent

Taiwan, China

ITEM	POLICY
● CBU Tariffs	→ 30 percent
● Parts Tariffs	→ 25 percent

Indonesia

ITEM	POLICY
● CBU Imports	→ prohibited
● CKD Tariffs	→ 100 percent
● Parts Tariffs (items not locally produced)	→ 5 percent
● Parts Tariffs (items locally produced)	→ 50 percent (calculated with reference to replacement part price)

Malaysia

ITEM	POLICY
● CBU Tariffs	→ zero (but excise duties from 140-300 percent of selling price)
● CKD for Tariffs	→ 40 percent
● CKD CV Tariffs	→ 5 percent

Thailand

ITEM	POLICY
● CBU Cars with Engines < 2.3 liters	→ prohibited
● Other CBU Vehicles	→ discriminatory internal taxes militate strongly against imports

Source: Authors' calculations.

V. *Strategic Policy Perspectives for Major Developing Countries*

The experiences in the selected countries are sufficiently diverse to suggest that strategic policy approaches should be "custom-made" within the overall drive towards international standards. The following sub-sections therefore deal with each country/region in turn. They are predicated on the idea that government and business together can produce results.

South America

The Transition to a Free Market System in the Automotive Industry

The history of automotive activity in South America has been marked by the persistent and occasionally negative involvement of government. In terms of equity participation governments have now withdrawn from the sector but their role in shaping trade policies, local content regulations, pricing of outputs and inputs, access to credit, and even the handling of the labor force remains extensive. Thus in Brazil more than 40 percent of the price paid by the consumer represents government revenue through taxes, a figure which is more than seven times the comparable number in the United States. Specific input problems with steel and informatics are a direct result of badly judged government interference in those sectors. Given the importance of the automotive industry in industrial activity in the region, there cannot be a transition to an open market system overnight. But it is imperative that the process begin at once and that it take place through a constant interaction and creation of mutual confidence between governments and firms.

Recent experiences in South America as well as in Mexico suggest a few guides to the key issues. First, price structures must be liberalized very quickly. Second, and partly as a consequence of the improvement in macroeconomic stability, credit conditions should be liberalized rapidly. Third, the maintenance of high local content levels is irrelevant if the industry is falling further behind with relation to world standards. Already the local content targets established in legislation are impossible to maintain; the new legal frameworks in Venezuela and Argentina embody much lower local content percentages as well as permit exports to compensate for local content (the 1989 automotive decree in Mexico includes provisions of this type). Fourth, trade policy changes may take longer to initiate but again the Mexican experience points the way with the emphasis on increasing competition through freer trade, thus encouraging efficient specialization within the Mexican market.

The dialogue necessary between the automotive firms and the government requires that the companies themselves clarify their position. In Venezuela the government effectively invited the industry to submit its own proposals, yet this has proved hard for the companies to do since there are strong conflicts of interest between different types of enterprise. Experience in other developing countries, including Republic of Korea, shows that automotive associations are defining their objectives more sharply and much more targeted work by them is fundamental to keeping pace with change. In South America the near future may well witness a number of adjustments of this kind.

The present period therefore needs to be one of rapid transition. The new paradigm focusses on world market standards, cooperation rather than conflict between governments and companies, a dramatic reduction in government intervention and a willingness to live from both exports and domestic sales. In the past many countries followed the same route of inward looking production whereas the outlook for the 1990s is that the accent will be on outward oriented activity.

Three types of automotive markets need to be distinguished, namely vehicle sales, original equipment manufacture and replacement markets. The first of these is totally controlled by multinational corporations. Exports will take place only if the international firms operating within South American countries choose to treat them as export sites. There were substantial vehicle exports from the region and within it during the 1980s, but also several instances where export models were withdrawn and sales were highly volatile. In the early 1990s Brazil's vehicle exports were below levels achieved early in the 1980s while Argentina has more or less ceased to be an export location.

Prospects for a recovery of South American exports in the near future are not good. The North American market is growing slowly in volume terms and switching to sophisticated models that are not manufactured in South America. At the lower end of the market, competition from Asian countries and Mexico is currently too strong for South America. Sales to Europe are not likely to be restarted since Volkswagen and Fiat are fully using their European networks to supply that market. Moreover, any transatlantic movements will come mainly from Japanese firms (primarily Honda) located in the United States. Although Africa is a small market compared to the OECD countries it could be a useful outlet for South American exports particularly since the two areas are geographically near. Both Brazil and Argentina have exported commercial vehicles there in the past and in spite of weak transport and communication difficulties between the two continents the effort should be maintained. In the Asian market South American countries are very badly placed due to the virtual nonexistence of Japanese producers within the region - in other words, intra company trade is not available. Those transpacific shipments which do go in a West to East direction originate from North America (including Mexico). Thus the implication is that intra regional trade will have to play a key part in export expansion.

These comments do not mean that vehicle sales have ceased to make key contributions to the automotive balance of trade. Indeed, export performance in commercial vehicles has been quite strong (though with fluctuations). The point is that the sustainability of the export push is particularly dependent on the major improvement in government policies and a corresponding response by companies.

As with vehicles, OEM component export sales are difficult to achieve unless there is a close tie-up with multinational corporations, whether the latter be vehicle or component manufacturers. At the moment, in-house production by vehicle firms is mostly located either in their home countries or in major affiliates. Where these firms contract production to outside companies, dealings are now centered on a much smaller number of first-tier suppliers than used to be the case. The big three producers in the United States are reported to be aiming for a 30 percent reduction in the number of outside suppliers between the early and late 1990s; VW has started a global purchasing organization with dealings in South America handled from Barcelona; and Nissan has begun to buy a few components from a firm in the Toyota family. Long-term contracts, meaning life of the model, are becoming the norm while design increasingly attempts to secure commonality of parts between models.

Thus the benefits from obtaining these markets are substantial but in practice only top rank suppliers can meet the tough criteria applied for selection. Arrangements tend to be with OECD firms, and South American producers are likely to come in mostly through subcontracting to them as second tier producers. Brazil's experience in OEM exports shows that upwards of 80 percent are made by foreign-owned companies with international reputations in the field. The shifting balance between component and vehicle producers requires constant investments in R and D by the former as well as permanent contact between the two. Furthermore the imperative of just-in-time delivery, though it does not exclude long distance deliveries, tends to create a preference for close proximity of suppliers and vehicle manufacturers. In short, OEM is not a market in which South American firms have many advantages.

Thus far relatively little attention has been paid to export opportunities for replacement markets. Estimates put the global retail value of that market at more than $400 billion a year, which translates to about $220 million at ex-factory prices. While some 40 to 45 percent of vehicle production is internationally traded, the proportion is much lower in the case of replacement parts. Yet several considerations suggest that South American countries might have advantages in export supply for these products. One argument is that production of many replacement and spare parts is not tied to vehicle manufacture, can be arranged on a bulk supply basis to distributors in major markets, and the quantities needed can be estimated from available statistics on breakdown rates for parts. A second point is that this market is much more open to medium and smaller size companies which do not require close links with multinational corporations. Neither of these points means that replacement markets export is easy or that quality levels can afford to be anything but the best. Rather, the argument is that the morphology of the market corresponds much more closely to the economic advantages which South American companies possess or can generate.

The behavior of parts imports in the United States suggests some of the opportunities. In the early 1990s purchases from the 11 leading supplier countries reached about $3 billion, a 60 percent increase as compared with the mid 1980s. Mexico, Brazil, Republic of Korea, and Taiwan, China together provided about 20 percent of the imports in the later period, a share rise of 2 percentage points. The key product groups from these emerging markets were ignition wiring, gas engines, brakes and parts, and parts of gas engines - in sum, these four items amounted to almost one third of all sales from the countries listed. Individual products of importance to Brazil include diesel engines (13 percent of Brazil's parts exports to the United States) as well as the items mentioned above. Thus despite the explosion in joint venture arrangements by Japanese component producers in the United States, there is still scope for exports to that market. While it may be impossible to devise a general strategy, plenty of specific opportunities seem to exist.

Ease of Cross Border Movement

Effective exports depend on good transport facilities, first rate communications (for example, telephone, fax), and minimal administrative and bureaucratic obstacles to trade. South American countries are not well placed in any of these dimensions. They are dependent on air services which have worsened rather than improved in recent years and maritime transport is also less frequent and for some routes more expensive than before. Throughout the region major investments to improve electronic communication facilities are only just being made and privatization of those sectors is still not widespread. This means that automotive companies cannot yet rely on world class linkages with potential clients. The bureaucratic hurdles are manifold, ranging from numerous tariff and non-tariff barriers through to substantial paperwork required to process foreign transactions.

These conditions are the product of the inward oriented attitudes which have prevailed in South America, attitudes which in their turn have led to a relative isolation of the region from international developments. The vicious circle of the past now has to be turned into a positive sequence of change and the first step must come from within the region. A firm commitment by governments and enterprises to encourage trade will make infrastructure investments worthwhile, and the presence of that infrastructure will in turn make exports relatively more profitable to undertake.

The Place of Exports in Corporate Policy

Vehicle exports of companies located in South America have varied widely in volume and destination. In some years exports have been negligible but in others they have been quite large. Exports have gone to countries across South America, North America, Western Europe and Africa yet with quantities altering substantially from year to year. A commitment to export requires explicit emphasis or consistent supply such that distributors and consumers abroad can rely on regular supplies and after-sales service. Otherwise, it is impossible to retain strong export competitiveness. Multinational corporations located in South America will only do this as long as this is part of their overall strategies and if they are confident that the region will provide a good environment for exports over a long period.

In the components field the volatility of sales between domestic and foreign destinations has been much less of a problem yet exports have not, for most companies, figured prominently in sales strategy. This situation must alter. The longer term survival of independent component producers is a function of their ability to meet and keep pace with international standards and that cannot be done unless firms are permanently involved in competition with high quality producers. For these companies also the development of exports becomes critical. Moreover, access to export markets permits realization of economies of scale. Since the rate of unit cost reduction consequent on bigger volumes is steep for many components, the advantages embrace price as well as quality. The only circumstances in which some firms may remain without external projection is if they are content to operate as second or third tier producers only. Although this position may be suitable for some firms it has the disadvantage that it restricts a firm to the lowest value added segments of production and leaves it highly vulnerable to sharp technological shifts.

Development of Export Markets

In every branch of automotive production the toughness of competition compels South American firms to explore and/or create opportunities in as many markets as possible. For vehicles and components there may be prospects on a wide geographical basis including within South America itself.

Regional trade complementation has been a constant theme of South American policy discussions but frequently has not proceeded much beyond the most limited arrangements. Protocol 21 of the Brazil/Argentina accords of 1986 started out with listings of more than 350 automotive components for trade between the two countries yet the numbers have been progressively reduced to only a fraction of the original figure. This reluctance to develop trade is not confined to South America as the persistent failures to expand automotive commerce among the ASEAN member countries testify. At the moment the most promising route seems to be for companies to make their own arrangements within the existing trade frameworks while pressuring their respective governments to liberalize the trade regime.

Most automotive companies in South America, except for the largest among them, do not devote sufficient resources to export market development in any region. The lack of information about volumes, prices, competitors, consumer preferences, marketing and distribution systems, and many other features of trade is extremely serious. The gap cannot be filled from one day to the next nor can immediate success be expected even when information is collected and analyzed. It follows that efforts must begin straightaway if results are to be seen by the second half of the decade.

There is scope for joint action through business associations and through government/business cooperation. In Canada, for example, both approaches have been used over several years and have yielded excellent results. The devices employed are familiar ones including regular appearances at industrial fairs, participation of component producers in trade missions, elaboration of data bases on targeted markets, and joint development of marketing arrangements. It appears that several Asian countries are using similar strategies; South America can do the same both in individual countries for a wide product range and across countries for closely defined items. Unless South American firms put themselves on the map for components, exports will be lost through default.

Private Sector Opportunities in Automotive Development in South America

In South America (as elsewhere) consumer choice will be given much greater scope than in earlier years. Automotive companies can respond to market signals, and incidentally improve their own profit performance, only if they supply the required products at the best quality and prices. The relative absence of competition in the past has not imposed sufficiently stringent requirements in this respect. From now on the companies must meet top standards.

In essence a first rate supply behavior represents the way in which the private sector can meet its obligations under a free market system. The advantages from cutting out government interference can only be passed on to the consumer if supply alters to match international standards. Fortunately international automotive industry conditions are such that this consequence is likely to follow quite quickly if South American countries switch their policies. The example of a multinational corporation plant in Mexico is eloquent: in 80 percent of recent company performance audits, this plant has been evaluated as the most efficient of the firm's units. Thus in the space of some 3-4 years the image of Mexico as merely an average quality production location has been altered -the investment and trade advantages of this transformation will accumulate in the future.

Speed of change requires firms to improve constantly not only their organization but also the standards of their staff. A consequence of the new environment discussed in this report is that South American companies will be compelled to invest heavily in on-the-job human resource improvement. The changes will go much beyond engineering and financial management. They encompass fresh attitudes towards consumers, new methods of marketing and distribution, and a readiness to explore new markets. Contrary to what is frequently supposed, the effect of a successful investment in human resources is likely to be an expansion of automotive employment and an increase in the positive impacts of the automotive industry on other economic sectors. In the late 1990s the wheel may come full circle as far as the role of the automotive industry in South American economies is concerned. The initial justification for investing in the industry was its beneficial impacts on employment, foreign exchange balances and the output of related sectors. However, government policies which at first fostered automotive industry growth remained rigid. With time, the attempt to achieve automotive industry aims within a protective environment and unstable macro economic conditions has been shown up as counterproductive. The about-turn to a stable economy with an open automotive sector can fulfill those original objectives.

Indian Subcontinent and China

Government Policy

Two forces have slowly started to push government policy concerns in the region, and ways for dealing with those concerns, in a direction consistent with recent moves elsewhere in the world. The first is the acceptance that standards of enterprise treatment and product quality should be compared at least on regional and preferably on international bases. Consequently, policies for reorganizing and upgrading the automotive industry within a region must be formulated with an eye to what happens outside. The second is the spread of information about alternatives. The presence of foreign firms and their representatives in the automotive industry associations in the region is one source of such information, but so is the wealth of material now coming from a variety of data banks and printed sources. The new "conventional wisdom" regarding automotive industry policy puts the accent on measures to encourage high quality standards, to balance foreign exchange through a mix of export promotion and import substitution, to orient the component branch to external operations, and to protect the environment from the nefarious effects of the automotive industry. The following paragraphs summarize the key points under each of these headings:

- *Quality Standards*

    Although protection against CBU imports is maintained, the new philosophy stresses that this cannot be used to permit poor quality in production. The fact that Japanese collaboration is dominant in the region, and that Japanese companies remain the pacesetters in all aspects of plant and system organization, helps to ensure that there is a drive for quality even if external competition does not exist. This stance does not weaken the traditional aim of high local content but often supports the establishment of realistic timetables, with the factor determining them being the rate of quality improvement. System organization, in particular the stress on JIT, has started to show up even in the regional distribution of component operations - in India today the new original equipment manufacture plants tend to be established in the vicinity of the Maruti assembly plant. Staff training is performed with international standards in mind, while the necessity of matching parts to foreign designs which incorporate many of the latest technical developments itself adds to the pressure.

- *Foreign Exchange*

    There cannot, as yet, be the same reliance on balancing of export sales against imports for each company which has characterized government policies in Latin America. But the need to encourage exports is gradually being recognized. One consequence is that governments must examine their tariffs on capital equipment imports, tariffs which raise production costs and therefore hinder exports. Another is that the component sector has to be improved, partly by government support for external fact-finding through education and promotional trips (including trade exhibitions). Persistence in such policies is essential lest manufacturers lose confidence in the seriousness with which the government takes the export drive. Once more treatment of local content is important. The critical observation is that whereas in the past there was held to be a tradeoff between a country's desire to raise local content and a foreign collaborator's interest in reducing it, the new circumstances of the world industry transform the picture. Companies will localize provided not only that they can maintain quality but, even more, develop export prospects. Hence local content policy, properly formulated, can now be seen in terms of symbiosis rather than conflict between governments and firms. By the same token, governments must encourage the spread of external networks, perhaps through their foreign collaborators, which can help to market automotive industry products. Finally, tax policy to support exports has to come in the early stages (when the export to output ratio is low) and not after the tough initial effort has already been made. Too often in the region tax breaks are given as a reward for export success rather than as a way of encouraging it.

- *Components*

The component industry internationally is also in the throes of a drive for rationalization, global reach, a heavy R and D effort, and the spread of subcontracting by the top layer producers. This means both risks and opportunities for Asian producers. The risks exist because of the possibility that transplants of these companies will move into developing country markets and thereby badly squeeze local companies unable to achieve the same standards. But the opportunities at present outweigh the risks. Like the assembly companies, component firms are looking for phased entry into markets where their knowledge is relatively limited and their practical experience minimal. Local government policy needs to be supportive of this by focusing on two points of importance to companies, namely, the recognition that genuine technology transfer can be encouraged, and that larger exports are possible. At present, the under-developed stage of policy towards components creates real openings for initiatives by the countries of the region. All of them have strong internal demand for replacement markets and original equipment manufacture, cost conditions are generally very competitive, and there is a rich experience of technology transfer. A move in this direction could be an excellent way to take advantage of current developments in the automotive industry. Indian component manufacturers have made remarkable progress in recent years and the recent liberalization provided additional impetus to exports. Between 1986-87 and 1992-93 output rose from Rs 12 billion to Rs 40 billion, 22 percent average annual growth, while exports rose from Rs 0.7 billion to Rs 5.3 billion, or 39 percent average annual growth. Most exports are for the replacement market but within the last three years or so several Indian companies are exporting original-equipment-manufacture to assemblers in Japan, Europe and the U.S. Exports have been boosted by the increasing number of alliances or technical collaboration agreements, well over two hundred at present, between Indian and foreign companies, many entailing off-take agreements. This growth is attributable to several factors, for example, rising disposable incomes, improved road infrastructure, greater experience by Indian companies and more focus on exports, but one of the necessary prerequisites has been the significant change in Government policies toward greater market orientation. Since international trade in components already exceeds trade in CBU and is much less protected, governments should be receptive to fresh ideas, especially in the aftermath of the successful Indian experience.

- *Environment*

In the OECD countries, the automotive industry has become, alongside the chemical industry, the principal target for government policy seeking to control and/or prevent environmental damage. Legislation and its enforcement are growing quickly and start to embrace a range of approaches which include both mandatory provisions and market oriented measures. At center stage is the total vehicle life cycle, that is, from design to disposal the vehicle will be affected by environmental policies. This concept raises the questions of who will bear the environment related costs at each stage and how those costs might affect both supply and demand. The key measures, and the responses to which they are giving rise in the production system, are:

- Fuel economy legislation, based around the CAFE schemes in force since the late 1960s in the United States, imposes significant financial penalties on companies which fail to provide a model mix that sufficiently limits fuel consumption. The legislation is becoming progressively tougher and is also sometimes employed as a protectionist device.

- Design of vehicles which can run on alternative fuels (methane, for example) or are powered by non-liquid means, for example, electric cars. Several examples of intra-urban use of the latter vehicles can be found in Europe, while early 1990s policies in California effectively guarantee these vehicles a significant share of sales by the turn of the century.

- A carbon tax, which would hit both the automotive industry and other sectors. This proposal, which was totally out of favor even a short time ago, now appears to be gaining support very fast (including from the automotive industry producers in OECD countries). Its imposition would, depending on the tax rate set, curtail the use of vehicles by a greater or lesser degree and therefore influence both vehicle design and purchase.

- Further increases in other automotive industry taxes so as to reduce environmental effects.

- Rigorous enforcement of regulations.

These matters acquired a global dimension through acceptance, in the second world climate conference held in late 1990, that vehicle use was an important factor contributing to the puncturing of the ozone layer and, therefore, to global warming. Moreover, the insistence that vehicles possess catalysators is just one illustration of how environment related laws can affect trade.

It appears that environmental policies are now starting to come under serious consideration in the developing Asian countries, driven still more by local than by international preoccupations. All of them are determined to promote fuel economy (though here the motives are also strongly influenced by the balance of payments) and would like to see atmospheric pollution reduced. Those policies will have to be fashioned with automotive industry associations taking an active and imaginative part in the deliberations. Maruti, for example, has already exported a few units to Europe where electric engines can be fitted to the light passenger car bodies, and it is known that some OECD firms might be interested in the production of newly designed bodies for alternative fuel vehicles in some of the Asian countries. Such mass market models might also be suitable for local consumption in the region. Hence it would be a mistake for environment policy to be tackled either in a narrow, internally focused way or limited to control measures without looking for ways that the region's automotive industry can be promoted through its awareness of the environment issue.

Regional Cooperation

This oft mooted, frequently frustrated theme might at last be an idea whose time has come as many multinational companies opt for a local presence in each region. Asian markets now have sufficient internal purchasing power to sustain sizeable regional consumption of vehicles. Governments in the region want to maintain a combination of protection and outward orientation, thereby offering credence to the idea of efficiency within a regional setting. The experience of some regional groupings (ASEAN), and the trends towards collaboration (strategic alliances) among companies, suggest more groups are now inclined to perceive the advantages rather than the risks of collaboration. This represents a radical change of attitude from earlier years. Furthermore, of the world's major automotive industry regions, Asia remains the one where most is to be done regarding cooperation.

In the early 1990s, DAF obtained approval within the ASEAN countries for a complementation scheme designed to produce 6,000 commercial vehicles. Its main features may serve as an example of what can be achieved:

- Equity, to the value of $200 million, would be provided by DAF, the European Community and the ASEAN member within each country.

- DAF guaranteed product buy-back, thereby giving the countries a safety net and encouraging each of them to participate.

- The allocation of activities among countries was guided by the technical level of partners, utilization of under-exploited capacity, and by the ability to convince governments of a win-win situation for everyone.

This approach started from the recognition by the European firm that Asia is a growth region, that some degree of market unification is desirable, and that little could be achieved unless local producers felt that risks are minimized in the early stages. The perception is important since it indicates that Asian countries have some assets around which good deals involving third parties can be constructed. The obvious areas where cooperation initiatives might be taken are in commercial vehicles, a less densely populated field than passenger cars, and in components. Given the sophisticated technology of the automotive industry, the involvement of an OECD partner wishing to improve global market share through locating in the region is an essential component of such a scheme. (The DAF deal in Asia was not implemented because of DAF's grave difficulties in its home, that is, European market).

Future Possibilities

Developing Asian countries have considerable prospects in the automotive industry. It remains a key manufacturing sector, the reductions in labor and material intensity of production have not diminished its relative importance, and even the thrust for global localization works to the advantage of the region. While various kinds of commercial vehicles are critical in overall sales, passenger cars are being taken up everywhere and all signs are that there is not only plenty of pent-up demand but that sustainable levels of consumption are also quite large. Policies are gradually becoming more flexible, oriented to taking advantage of options rather than imposing further controls, while the scale diseconomies which tended to discourage production in the past no longer appear to set such heavy unit cost penalties as they once did. There is, moreover, a better atmosphere of dialogue between producing firms (including component manufacturers) and governments than has existed at any time before. In brief: the conditions are ripe to undertake fresh ventures.

The areas which could be explored include:

- Export markets for components. The issues include linkages with already established international distribution networks, exports via assembly firms already collaborating in the region, promotion of trade fairs, and changes in government policies to facilitate equipment and other imports needed to help production for export.

- Trade development through contacts with companies from the exporting country already established abroad. The largest Asian countries have large numbers of citizens abroad, many of whom could help in export promotion and distribution.

- Arrangement of foreign collaborations such that brand name use also takes cognisance of the Asian producer.

- Steps to encourage domestic demand still more, such that it drives the industry forward. This, in turn, will attract more foreign collaboration and thus increase the chances that quality and scale of output increase export opportunities.

The automotive industry in Asia now has a real chance to create the dynamism which corresponds to the region's place in the world economy. If the world is splitting into fast and slow growing regions, at the same time that it is becoming more interlinked, then Asia is very much in the vanguard. The essence of the image must be an openness of attitude (often confused with the openness of markets, though the two are not synonymous) sustained by a commitment to strong performance. The examples of Mexico and Republic of Korea show how quickly the automotive industry can be turned into a dynamic sector once the attitudinal openness is there for all to see. The history of the automotive industry repeatedly demonstrates that the growth possibilities for those committed to quality output are highly attractive. Developing Asia is now in an excellent position to provide another demonstration.

Indonesia and the ASEAN Countries

The Constraints on Growth

There is no doubt that the automotive industry labors under some severe handicaps of "context" in Indonesia. The geography of the islands allied with the difficulties in constructing adequate road arteries certainly limits vehicle use. Even if additional substantial investments in roads were to be made, much would still be required with regard to service and maintenance networks. Private investments in the automotive industry have in recent years been rendered more risky by the high and volatile interest rates along with a number of administrative regulations which further increase the cost of capital. The accent on developing a few branches of heavy industry has meant that firms can obtain some key materials locally yet are burdened through the prices they must pay for them and/or by inferior quality.

While these difficulties are real and significant, the primary obstacles to growth of an efficient automotive industry are those coming through government policy. At the core of the debate is the belief that Indonesia can adopt a path which is markedly different from that followed by others. In certain industrial sectors a pronounced degree of individuality in product, and perhaps even process, may be consistent with economical manufacture - but the automotive industry is not one of those sectors. It needs constant dialogue among all interested groups. It requires acceptance of the prevailing standards of sectoral efficiency if it is to make its contribution to development and it cannot do without the impetus provided by domestic, and not just export, demand. It can operate efficiently only when relations among joint venture partners are stable and based on a common commitment to reach world standards and not just juggle local forms of protection to yield profits to the few while raising costs for the many. Indonesia has every chance to develop the automotive industry successfully provided it works with the requirements just sketched rather than against them.

The Trends That Matter

The perception of the automotive industry most likely to nurture sound policies centers around the following trends:

- Constant relocation and internationalization of the automotive industry, both in CBU and components, creates numerous opportunities for successful new collaboration. One of the great mistakes is to imagine that the sector's structure is rigid and amenable only to slow change.

- Competition among firms in all branches of the industry (passenger cars, commercial vehicles of various kinds, original equipment manufacture and replacement market parts) throughout the world is so intense that the "regions of influence" pattern currently dominating world automotive industry can be altered rapidly.

- It is incorrect to believe that a strong automotive industry (and even a fully integrated automotive industry) can only be built by working backwards from vehicle assembly. That paradigm has governed all policies in most developing countries over the past 40 years. But strong efforts in well chosen areas of component manufacture can just as well serve as the core from which everything else is made.

- No policy towards the automotive industry will permit a wide range of objectives to be satisfied simultaneously. Priorities have to be set and maintained - if production is efficient, a virtuous circle can be set in motion.

Guiding Principles for Policy Formulation

Given the perception just defined, the way in which policies are created and operated becomes critical. Key points to consider would be:

- Automotive industry policy is neither a series of decrees handed down from government nor a mere result of internal debates among a few assemblers and one or two Ministries. It is a process which compels the participation of all branches of the industry on the production side, of consumer groups of diverse kinds, and (today more than ever) of persons with knowledge of environmental and related issues. The initiatives for changes in policy may come from any of these sources.

- While the policy agreement must be adhered to, and frequent manipulation of measures does not improve confidence, the speed of change today is such that policies have to be designed with change factors built in. Under no circumstances should any interest group be able to appeal to a policy as if it were sacrosanct or to change it for its own narrow interests.

- Prior announcement of draft policies followed by adequate time for public debate has much to commend it. Though conflict is a normal part of the process, and in this sense to be encouraged rather than disguised, the aim must be to create consensus around the directions of change and the instruments for promoting it. Once policies are announced, reasonable time for adjustment must be allowed to interested firms. However, it must be made clear that this in fact is a period to adjust and not for further lobbying.

- The relationships between what is done in the automotive industry and the development prospects of other branches suggest that the automotive industry should not implicitly be assigned a priority at the expense of other parts of the industrial sector.

Among the many ideas which will likely appear as the automotive industry policy debate gathers force in Indonesia, the following points certainly will be on the action list:

- Analysis of market opportunities, at home and abroad. One of the major weaknesses as of now is the absence of information collected, analyzed and used as a basis for action by Indonesian groups in the automotive industry. Without that the only stimuli for change will be the internal crises of industry branches (which is no basis from which to launch fresh endeavors) or proposals advanced by external groups. Though the latter may well illustrate advantages for Indonesia, it is extremely unlikely they will cover the spectrum of new opportunities for the country.

- Analysis of policy trends elsewhere. Since one of the features of the automotive industry today is the application of global best practice to policy as well as production, it is vital that policy monitoring be used. The groups who do this should be composed of a range of interests and not confined to government officials.

- Utilization of technical services, and perhaps ultimately the capital involvement, of international bodies such as IFC. Their knowledge of developments elsewhere gives them a good position from which to advise while their operating tenets that all projects should be technically feasible, economically viable, financially profitable and environmentally sound, provide criteria against which assessments within Indonesia can be tested.

Indonesia is by no means alone in being confronted with an automotive industry policy challenge. But it does have its own industry history, resource set and development horizons. They lead to greater opportunities on some fronts along with larger risks on others. The ideal response to Indonesia's own opportunity/risk cluster is to stimulate domestic demand and encourage much greater competition in all branches of manufacture. The size and variety of Indonesia's market are a powerful guarantee this approach will yield returns.

Central Europe

The Government Vacuum

Given the failures of the past, it is scarcely surprising that government is trying to withdraw from many areas where previously it determined events. Unfortunately, the pullback comes fastest in those areas where prudent government presence is necessary, and slowest in the issues where it should be removed. There is little capability to support retraining of staff, no fresh investment to support infrastructure, and no clear reorganization of trade flows. The hope appears to be that, just as in the area of macro economic affairs, technical and to some extent financial assistance from abroad will take care of things. This has created a void which in fact complicates the tasks in those realms where the State should be withdrawing its presence rapidly, viz. direct involvement in production, foreign trade and internal distribution.

Partly as a result of the sudden withdrawal by governments from areas where the private sector cannot possibly fill the vacuum, at least in the near to medium term, individual company prospects vary a great deal. Some Czech and Slovak firms are optimistic, either because foreign commitments are secured (Skoda, BAZ) or because past activities had allowed them to specialize in manufacture where markets abroad were still achievable (Tatra). The Hungarian bus producer, Ikarus, nevertheless faces serious problems since its marketing was closely tied to the former CMEA structure; the inability to cope with the virtual elimination of those outlets has left the firm in a difficult position. In Poland the situation likewise is mixed in that the Fiat commitment to FSM (and in particular the decision to make it the source for the Cinquecento) seems to suggest a reasonable future, as does the GM investment in FSO. But so far there are few signs of major commitments to the component business (Ford's manufacture of ignition coils and fuel pumps in Hungary is an exception) while the promotion of foreign trade for smaller firms

45

is likely to take some reorganization. In all of this the behavior of governments has been hesitant and, on the whole, not encouraging for the parties to negotiations.

Creating an Automotive Industry Business Context

Opportunities seem to outpace realities in Central Europe. To try and narrow the gap a number of points should be kept in mind:

- Amidst all the hectic activity from day to day, a new automotive industry cannot be built in anything other than a fairly long time horizon. The persistence and determination required must come from three key economic agents, viz. the automotive industry firms themselves, the government and the financial institutions. Thus far there are some signs (through foreign direct investment) that this kind of perspective may begin to take root in the sector itself. Similar indicators from the other two agents are far less visible.

- The creation of dense networks for dialogue is essential. Nowhere in Central Europe are there the industry and trade associations which play such a vital role elsewhere. Recent efforts in Indonesia, for instance, have begun to show the value of bringing together firms, particularly in the component field, so that they can share knowledge of markets and customers, develop group training programs, and be in a position to engage in dialogue with the government. Yet another of the consequences of the government pullback is that firms must take the initiative in dialogue with the ministries, persuading them of the value in promotional actions. At the moment the ministries seem most worried about appearing satisfactory to foreign assistance groups while the automotive industry firms are most concerned about the image they give to foreign automotive industry enterprises. While this may be understandable it is not acceptable as a permanent state of affairs.

- VW noted how its vendor conferences have helped to create confidence and strength among component producers. This approach could well be followed more extensively in the region.

- The emphasis on managing companies effectively entails, among other things, creation of a work ethic which puts quality, continuous improvement, and performance at the top of the list. Hard though this is, Central Europe is not the only region facing the problem and may have some chances to proceed more quickly than elsewhere. Incentive structures must be managed consistently with this activity.

- Technical cooperation with foreign firms takes on a new perspective given the changed conditions within Central Europe and in the automotive industry as a whole. Licensing, for example, will in future involve patents but the likelihood that know-how will be available is not great. Some foreign firms, such as GKN, now insist on some equity holdings where there are licenses at stake. Effective linkages with external developments require the automotive industry firms to stay abreast of such shifts of technology supplier behavior.

- There must be a domestic commitment to training and learning. The short run hope is clearly that in-plant efforts will take care of problems and indeed perhaps that is so. But the need for broader investment in training is crucial. In this respect Central Europe may again reap some benefit from the Europe-wide changes in education/training and stricter work attitudes.

Bibliography

Asociación de Fábricantes de Automotores, "La Industria Automotriz Argentina: Motor de la Recuperación Económica", Buenos Aires, October 1992.

---. "Industria Automotriz Argentina", Buenos Aires, December 1991.

ANFAVEA, "The Brazilian Automotive Industry 1991", Sao Paulo, 1992.

Automotive Component Manufacturers Association of India, "Recent Developments in the Indian Auto Component Sector", New Delhi, December 1992.

Berry, S., V. Grilli and F. López de Silenes, *The Automobile Industry and the Mexico-US Free Trade Agreement*, NBER Working Paper 1452, August 1992.

Booz-Allen and Hamilton, Inc., *Final Report: Automotive Industry Study*, June 1992.

Economist Intelligence Unit. "The Motor Industries of the European Region: Western Europe, Eastern Europe and Mediterranean Countries", May 1992.

---. "The Motor Industries of Japan, South Korea and the Pacific Rim Countries", May 1992.

---. "The Motor Industry of South America", May 1992.

---. "The Motor Industries of India and China", May 1992.

IFC, Economics Department. "A Report on the Automotive Industry Seminar Sao Paulo, Brazil", May 1990.

---. "A Report on the Automotive Industry Seminar New Delhi, India", December 1990.

---. "A Report on the Automotive Industry Seminar Jakarta, Indonesia", May 1991.

---. "A Report on the Automotive Industry Seminar for Central and Eastern Europe, Budapest, Hungary", November 1991.

---. *Active Investment Report*, June 1992.

Karlin, A., "Automotive Industry Review", IFC Memorandum, December 1992.

Karmokolias, Y. *Automotive Industry Trends and Prospects for Investment in Developing Countries*, IFC Discussion Paper 7, 1990.

Maruti Udyog Ltd., "Recent Government Policies and Regulations Affecting the Automotive Industry in India", Communication to IFC, December 1992.

O'Brien, Peter, *The Automotive Industry in the Developing Countries: Risks and Opportunities in the 1990s*, London, 1989.

---. *The Prospects for Collaboration in Trade and Production Between Developed and Developing Countries in the Automotive Industry*, Geneva, 1989.

---. "New Perspectives on the Automotive Industry in South America", Washington, May 1990.

---. "The Automotive Industry in Developing Asian Countries: Issues and Prospects", Washington, January 1991.

---. "Automotive Policy at the Crossroads", Geneva, May 1991.

---. "Automotive Industry and Automotive Policy: Directions of Change", Jakarta, May 1991.

---. "Tackling the Transition: The Problems and Prospects for the Automotive Industry in Central and Eastern Europe", Geneva, December 1991.

---. "The Government's Role in a Market Economy", Budapest, November 1991.

---. "Automotive Industry: The Permanent Revolution", in *Industry on the Move*, ILO, Geneva, November 1992.

República de Argentina, *Decreto 2677 de 20 de diciembre de 1991*, Buenos Aires, December 1991.

Snowdon, M., "Development Opportunities for the Eastern European Automotive Industry", Budapest, November 1991.

UNCTC, *Foreign Direct Investment and Industrial Restructuring in Mexico*, New York, 1992.

Distributors of World Bank Publications

ARGENTINA
Carlos Hirsch, SRL
Galeria Guemes
Florida 165, 4th Floor-Ofc. 453/465
1333 Buenos Aires

**AUSTRALIA, PAPUA NEW GUINEA,
FIJI, SOLOMON ISLANDS,
VANUATU, AND WESTERN SAMOA**
D.A. Information Services
648 Whitehorse Road
Mitcham 3132
Victoria

AUSTRIA
Gerold and Co.
Graben 31
A-1011 Wien

BANGLADESH
Micro Industries Development
Assistance Society (MIDAS)
House 5, Road 16
Dhanmondi R/Area
Dhaka 1209

Branch offices:
Pine View, 1st Floor
100 Agrabad Commercial Area
Chittagong 4100

BELGIUM
Jean De Lannoy
Av. du Roi 202
1060 Brussels

CANADA
Le Diffuseur
151A Boul. de Mortagne
Boucherville, Québec
J4B 5E6

Renouf Publishing Co.
1294 Algoma Road
Ottawa, Ontario
K1B 3W8

CHILE
Invertec IGT S.A.
Av. Santa Maria 6400
Edificio INTEC, Of. 201
Santiago

CHINA
China Financial & Economic
Publishing House
8, Da Fo Si Dong Jie
Beijing

COLOMBIA
Infoenlace Ltda.
Apartado Aereo 34270
Bogota D.E.

COTE D'IVOIRE
Centre d'Edition et de Diffusion
Africaines (CEDA)
04 B.P. 541
Abidjan 04 Plateau

CYPRUS
Center of Applied Research
Cyprus College
6, Diogenes Street, Engomi
P.O. Box 2006
Nicosia

DENMARK
SamfundsLitteratur
Rosenoerns Allé 11
DK-1970 Frederiksberg C

DOMINICAN REPUBLIC
Editora Taller, C. por A.
Restauración e Isabel la Católica 309
Apartado de Correos 2190 Z-1
Santo Domingo

EGYPT, ARAB REPUBLIC OF
Al Ahram
Al Galaa Street
Cairo

The Middle East Observer
41, Sherif Street
Cairo

FINLAND
Akateeminen Kirjakauppa
P.O. Box 128
SF-00101 Helsinki 10

FRANCE
World Bank Publications
66, avenue d'Iéna
75116 Paris

GERMANY
UNO-Verlag
Poppelsdorfer Allee 55
53115 Bonn

HONG KONG, MACAO
Asia 2000 Ltd.
46-48 Wyndham Street
Winning Centre
7th Floor
Central Hong Kong

HUNGARY
Foundation for Market Economy
Dombovari Ut 17-19
H-1117 Budapest

INDIA
Allied Publishers Private Ltd.
751 Mount Road
Madras - 600 002

Branch offices:
15 J.N. Heredia Marg
Ballard Estate
Bombay - 400 038

13/14 Asaf Ali Road
New Delhi - 110 002

17 Chittaranjan Avenue
Calcutta - 700 072

Jayadeva Hostel Building
5th Main Road, Gandhinagar
Bangalore - 560 009

3-5-1129 Kachiguda
Cross Road
Hyderabad - 500 027

Prarthana Flats, 2nd Floor
Near Thakore Baug, Navrangpura
Ahmedabad - 380 009

Patiala House
16-A Ashok Marg
Lucknow - 226 001

Central Bazaar Road
60 Bajaj Nagar
Nagpur 440 010

INDONESIA
Pt. Indira Limited
Jalan Borobudur 20
P.O. Box 181
Jakarta 10320

IRAN
Kowkab Publishers
P.O. Box 19575-511
Tehran

IRELAND
Government Supplies Agency
4-5 Harcourt Road
Dublin 2

ISRAEL
Yozmot Literature Ltd.
P.O. Box 56055
Tel Aviv 61560

ITALY
Licosa Commissionaria Sansoni SPA
Via Duca Di Calabria, 1/1
Casella Postale 552
50125 Firenze

JAPAN
Eastern Book Service
Hongo 3-Chome, Bunkyo-ku 113
Tokyo

KENYA
Africa Book Service (E.A.) Ltd.
Quaran House, Mfangano Street
P.O. Box 45245
Nairobi

KOREA, REPUBLIC OF
Pan Korea Book Corporation
P.O. Box 101, Kwangwhamun
Seoul

Korean Stock Book Centre
P.O. Box 34
Yeoeido
Seoul

MALAYSIA
University of Malaya Cooperative
Bookshop, Limited
P.O. Box 1127, Jalan Pantai Baru
59700 Kuala Lumpur

MEXICO
INFOTEC
Apartado Postal 22-860
14060 Tlalpan, Mexico D.F.

NETHERLANDS
De Lindeboom/InOr-Publikaties
P.O. Box 202
7480 AE Haaksbergen

NEW ZEALAND
EBSCO NZ Ltd.
Private Mail Bag 99914
New Market
Auckland

NIGERIA
University Press Limited
Three Crowns Building Jericho
Private Mail Bag 5095
Ibadan

NORWAY
Narvesen Information Center
Book Department
P.O. Box 6125 Etterstad
N-0602 Oslo 6

PAKISTAN
Mirza Book Agency
65, Shahrah-e-Quaid-e-Azam
P.O. Box No. 729
Lahore 54000

PERU
Editorial Desarrollo SA
Apartado 3824
Lima 1

PHILIPPINES
International Book Center
Suite 1703, Cityland 10
Condominium Tower 1
Ayala Avenue, H.V. dela
Costa Extension
Makati, Metro Manila

POLAND
International Publishing Service
Ul. Piekna 31/37
00-677 Warzawa

For subscription orders:
IPS Journals
Ul. Okrezna 3
02-916 Warszawa

PORTUGAL
Livraria Portugal
Rua Do Carmo 70-74
1200 Lisbon

SAUDI ARABIA, QATAR
Jarir Book Store
P.O. Box 3196
Riyadh 11471

**SINGAPORE, TAIWAN,
MYANMAR,BRUNEI**
Gower Asia Pacific Pte Ltd.
Golden Wheel Building
41, Kallang Pudding, #04-03
Singapore 1334

SOUTH AFRICA, BOTSWANA
For single titles:
Oxford University Press
Southern Africa
P.O. Box 1141
Cape Town 8000

For subscription orders:
International Subscription Service
P.O. Box 41095
Craighall
Johannesburg 2024

SPAIN
Mundi-Prensa Libros, S.A.
Castello 37
28001 Madrid

Librería Internacional AEDOS
Consell de Cent, 391
08009 Barcelona

SRI LANKA AND THE MALDIVES
Lake House Bookshop
P.O. Box 244
100, Sir Chittampalam A.
Gardiner Mawatha
Colombo 2

SWEDEN
For single titles:
Fritzes Fackboksforetaget
Regeringsgatan 12, Box 16356
S-103 27 Stockholm

For subscription orders:
Wennergren-Williams AB
P. O. Box 1305
S-171 25 Solna

SWITZERLAND
For single titles:
Librairie Payot
Case postale 3212
CH 1002 Lausanne

For subscription orders:
Librairie Payot
Service des Abonnements
Case postale 3312
CH 1002 Lausanne

THAILAND
Central Department Store
306 Silom Road
Bangkok

**TRINIDAD & TOBAGO, ANTIGUA
BARBUDA, BARBADOS,
DOMINICA, GRENADA, GUYANA,
JAMAICA, MONTSERRAT, ST.
KITTS & NEVIS, ST. LUCIA,
ST. VINCENT & GRENADINES**
Systematics Studies Unit
#9 Watts Street
Curepe
Trinidad, West Indies

UNITED KINGDOM
Microinfo Ltd.
P.O. Box 3
Alton, Hampshire GU34 2PG
England